Finding Your Voice

Finding Your Voice

Engaging Confidently in All God Created You to Be

JENNIFER TURNER

Foreword by Mandy Smith

RESOURCE *Publications* · Eugene, Oregon

FINDING YOUR VOICE
Engaging Confidently in All God Created You to Be

Copyright © 2021 Jennifer Turner. All rights reserved. Except for brief quotations in critical publications or reviews, no part of this book may be reproduced in any manner without prior written permission from the publisher. Write: Permissions, Wipf and Stock Publishers, 199 W. 8th Ave., Suite 3, Eugene, OR 97401.

Resource Publications
An Imprint of Wipf and Stock Publishers
199 W. 8th Ave., Suite 3
Eugene, OR 97401

www.wipfandstock.com

PAPERBACK ISBN: 978-1-6667-0580-5
HARDCOVER ISBN: 978-1-6667-0581-2
EBOOK ISBN: 978-1-6667-0582-9

08/02/21

All Scripture quotations unless otherwise indicated are taken from THE HOLY BIBLE, NEW INTERNATIONAL VERSION®, NIV® Copyright © 1973, 1978, 1984, 2011 by Biblica, Inc.™ Used by permission. All rights reserved worldwide.

Some Scripture quotations are from *The Message*. Copyright © 1993, 1994, 1995, 1996, 2000, 2001, 2002. Used by permission of NavPress Publishing Group.

Grateful thanks is extended to the Iona Community and the Wild Goose Resource group for permission to use a verse of "The Summons" by John L. Bell and Graham Maule. © 1987, Wild Goose Resource Group c/o Iona Community. Administered in Australia and New Zealand by Willow Publishing Pty Ltd. www.willowpublishing.com.au Administered in North America by GIA Publications, Inc. www.giamusic.com Used with permission. All rights reserved.

Thank you also to the Dayspring Community for the poem by Helen Maiden, "Aged Yet Most Colourful," from *Epiphanies of Grace: Poems and Psalms from the Dayspring Community.* Holliday, Brian and Beth Roberton, eds. Dianella, Western Australia: Dayspring, 2011. www.dayspring.org.au Used with permission.

Four articles by the author published in the Australian quarterly journal, *Zadok Perspectives,* have been used in part in this book. *Zadok Perspectives* is now published by *Ethos: Evangelical Alliance Centre for Christianity and Society,* Melbourne, Australia. www.ethos.org.au

For the three wonderful daughters-in-law our sons have given us
Vicki, Kristy, and Wendy

Contents

Foreword by Mandy Smith		ix
Acknowledgments		xi
An Invitation		xiii
1	Start by Telling your Story	1
2	Listen to Your Life	15
3	Simply Yourself, More Than Yourself	29
4	Leaving Home	41
5	Imposter Syndrome	53
6	Body People, Resurrection People	65
7	Beautiful with God's Beauty	79
8	Beyond Shame	96
9	Invitations for this Season of your Life	109
10	The Courage of Faith	123
Epilogue: Mary's Story		135
Bibliography		139

Foreword

Two years ago, I was healed quite unexpectedly in a busy hotel lobby. I was chatting with a mentor and suddenly, with purpose and affection, she held my face in her hands and said, "Mandy, you are so beautiful!" I do not know how she did it, but I received it as the affection of God. And something remarkable became possible. Not only did I see God in a new way—as the kind of being who might hold my face and tell me I am beautiful—but I saw myself in a new way. If this warm, maternal act of affection—something often seen as insignificant, subjective, feminine emotion—helped me know God's love in new ways, could it be that my own acts of warm, maternal affection also had this kind of power in the lives of others?

Last month I wrapped up thirteen years of ministry at a church I love. To send me off the leaders organized a time of story-telling and for several hours I was treated to many stories of how people saw God in me. Thankfully, I had received many notes of encouragement over the years but something about these stories went deeper, flooding my senses to find a place beyond my own fears of inadequacy and unhealthy people-pleasing tendencies. In these stories, people I love and trust described events I remembered and a person I recognise as myself—a creative, emotional, encourager who makes space and whose hugs apparently smell like essential oils. And then they went on to say, "That person showed me God and I've never been the same since." Beyond "thanks for doing a nice thing," these stories opened my heart and imagination to the possibility that these folks had experienced something new about God because of ordinary ways I was learning to live my faith among them. It was not until after the gathering that I noticed new kinds of healing in myself. Suddenly my prayers seemed to be directed to a new part of God, someone who was more like me than God had ever seemed before. Although it felt like heresy, I found myself asking, "Could God be like me?" Not like me *only* but like me *also*. I was familiar with a well-meaning but distant father God. But this new presence I sensed from God was the kind of being who holds my face, warmly says,

"You're beautiful" then gives me a hug which smells like essential oils. That's the kind of pastor I am.[1] Could it be that God, while being all the familiar things, might also be like this? Like me?

I tell these stories because as I read Jennifer Turner's words, I am invited into the same kind of space as in that hotel lobby and in that send-off story session. Dr Turner writes with warmth and wisdom, pastoring us from the pages. And as we have the opportunity to receive her voice in this way, we are presented not only with new ideas but new imaginations. Her unique pastoral voice allows us both to see God in a new way and to see how God might want to be revealed through us in a new way. God embodies something unique in the bodies of his daughters!

Jennifer describes this dynamic herself: "When I was eventually in a pastoral position . . . I discovered that my visibility had good consequences for others that I had not anticipated. Women said to me: 'Because you are there, I am learning to feel better about myself. It makes a difference.' Release becomes a possibility through positive identification with someone who represents us." What was possible in the past through her pastoral ministry becomes possible now, in her writing ministry.

What a wonderful possibility—that as more and more women embrace who they truly are and how God wants to be revealed through their unique experience, personality and voice, something new is birthed in the church and the world. Not for the sakes of these women (although they will certainly be blessed) and not because it is fair (although it may bring about more justice in the church and world) but because the world needs to see God in these ways. And as each of us steps with more courage into our voice and calling, learning from the mess and missteps, may the world see the richness of the face of God, may they know a God who in addition to all the usual images of God, also holds their face with tenderness, expresses deep welcome and maybe even is a little bit like them.

MANDY SMITH, Pastor and Author (*The Vulnerable Pastor* and *Unfettered*)

---

1. Of course, not all women have a traditionally maternal or physically affectionate way. May God also be revealed to and through them in their unique personalities and gifts.

Acknowledgments

A BIG THANK YOU to those who have helped along the way to this book being published. It represents a lifetime of experience made richer by friends and family. Many of you will recognize yourselves and the experiences we have shared in these pages. I am especially appreciative of your companionship and support as I have travelled to distant continents or found myself on new frontiers. I look forward to many more journeys in your company in the future.

Thank you to my colleague Joy Eichhorn who received every chapter from me as I wrote it and provided great perspective from her years as a psychologist.

My husband also read those chapters thoroughly with red pen in hand, and gave me back pages that "bled" profusely! For that I am grateful but even more so for his continuing belief in me and his encouragement.

Other friends and colleagues commented on chapters that reflected their expertise and experience. A special *thank you* to Yvette, Briallen, Kiralee, Tamzen and of course, to Mandy Smith.

An Invitation

The Lord God said:
I myself will dream a dream within you.
Good dreams come from me you know.
    My dreams seem impossible,
    not too practical, not for the cautious man or woman
    a little risky sometimes, a trifle brash perhaps.
Some of my friends prefer to rest comfortably
    in sounder sleep, with visionless eyes.
But, from those who share my dreams
    I ask a little patience, a little humour,
    some small courage
    and a listening heart—
I will do the rest.

—Charles Péguy (1873–1914)[2]

Do you hear God's dream for you? Do you welcome an invitation to know yourself and enjoy the delight your Creator has in you? Do you want to follow Jesus into the future with confidence?

    Whether you are a woman or a man starting on the journey or at a midpoint anticipating a change of direction, or even thinking you see the end, I write to encourage you to engage fully and boldly in the life that lies ahead of you. I want you to relish honest conversations around your pilgrimage with others who do life with you. But most of all, I want to remind you that the God who made you and redeemed you, longs for you to flourish in your

---

2. Charles Péguy was a noted French poet, socialist, activist and essayist. Late in life he embraced Christianity and his poetry from that time reflects his posture of hope.

life with Jesus. It is what God intended for you from your very creation. It is God's dream for you. I hope it is your dream too.

This journey towards longed-for fullness of life and service I am calling *Finding Your Voice*. Nancy Beach[3] uses this expression to describe the process of understanding yourself and your contribution around the table of leadership—becoming comfortable and participating fully, in joining your voice to the conversation. We women have often experienced being invisible, and so we grow afraid of being fully present in many settings. Consciously, or unconsciously, we hide who we are and what we can do because we feel our very being is unacceptable to those who hold the power and set the standards.

Even more, as women we are aware of how different we sound to the expected tone and presence of authority. *Finding your voice* is an affirmation that the Creator worked purposely in making and gifting each one of us with our voice. It is that voice, that self, God invites you to uncover and offer to the world in service as well as in self-expression.

Sometimes we resent the choices we have had to make in life. Yet we feel guilty about wanting more, hearing the ancient word, "Thou shalt not covet" in that guilty feeling. Or we know that adding anything more to what we are doing now is not practical—indeed life seems already an impossible juggling act.

A JOURNEY OF MANY SMALL STEPS

This is why *finding your voice* is a journey of many small steps. It does not happen all at once and involves letting go of things that blind or bind—attitudes to yourself or your body, for example, and to the burdens you try to carry alone. These important steps and the opportunities they bring we will consider one by one in the chapters that follow.

Many of the tools for this longed-for growth in self-awareness and service have already been given to us. Telling our story to an empathetic listener is one. It encourages us to notice where God is at work in our life. Recognising the season of life we are in—its tasks and its opportunities—is another that we will consider towards the end of the book. This is often very freeing in itself, but it can also open us to new ways to express our voice.

---

3. Beach, *Gifted to Lead*, 107. The expression comes from research by Jane Stephens on how women leaders communicate. Stephens says: Voice is "about learning to get in touch, listen to and trust your own instincts . . . Born at the intersection of tentativity and certainty, it requires both vulnerability and presence." Nancy Beach applies this to women working in the church.

These crucial steps to flourishing are for both women and men. I strongly recommend them.

A STRETCHING JOURNEY

I personally have discovered the process of finding my voice both comforting and stretching. My parents were very supportive and had high expectations for me academically as a woman. They had bravely modelled following God at considerable personal cost over the years and had every confidence that I would be an independent and competent adult. But it was not long before I discovered that there were limitations to what I could *be* and *do* because I was a woman, and a married one at that.

When I was rejected from a higher study program in the United States in the 1960s on the grounds of those personal characteristics, it was in words that an academic institution would never use today because they would be accused of discrimination. However, I accepted it as God's direction for my life and enjoyed a wonderful and enriching six further years in the country gaining wide experience as a consultant town planner before my husband and I returned to Australia.

When later I found the same barriers to Christian women using their God-given gifts in the church, it caused considerably more pain. At the time, I was writing Bible study group material for our church on the spiritual gifts that the Apostle Paul describes as enriching the church and enhancing its ministry to the world. It was clear in the three key Bible passages I was examining (1 Cor 12, Rom 12, Eph 4) that there was no hint of gender bias in his descriptions of the gifts given, or who receives them. This period of my life coincided with our children becoming more independent and I was exploring where to invest my newly available time and energy. I knew it should be guided by an understanding of my natural and spiritual gifts. At that transition point in my life and many times since, as I have pondered the next step, I have been helped by Elizabeth O'Connor's words, "To surrender to what is written into the fabric of our lives is to surrender to the will of God."[4]

Ah yes, God acts with great purpose, written in the fabric of our life. The Creator has known us from our mother's womb and invites us to examine all the dimensions of our lives, entering with freedom and courage into their fulness. Finding self-acceptance and our God-given voice is a response of obedience to the God who loves us and is transforming us. We dare not neglect its call.

---

4. O'Connor, *Journey Inward, Journey Outward*, 34.

PURSUING THE SELF

This self we come to know and accept is always the self-in-relationship—connected first of all with our Creator. Psychologist David Benner in encouraging the pursuit of the self has written, "Deep knowing of self gives opportunity for deep knowing of God, just as deep knowing of God gives opportunity for deep knowing of self."[5] This is not uniformity, a squashing of our individuality, but a full blossoming of it. It is a life-long adventure. Brené Brown calls it braving the wilderness of uncertainty, vulnerability, and criticism. We do not know where it will take us or the challenges along the way, but I write to share with you what I have discovered on this journey and the delights of its discoveries. I long for you to have the joy of finding your voice too.

But there is a problem. Many of us were taught from childhood that focusing on ourselves is wrong. We were told to be more concerned for others than for ourselves. J.O.Y. Jesus first; Others next; Yourself last. Pondering this, I made a list of the writers who had been most influential in my early days. I discovered it was those who honestly told the story of their spiritual journey and what they had learned about God and themselves along the way who spoke most powerfully to me. Names such as Isabel Kuhn, Amy Carmichael and Catherine Marshall came to mind; later Joyce Huggett and Rebecca Manley Pippert. More recently it has been Nancy Beach, Mandy Smith, and Anna McGahan. They describe considerable challenges, requiring courage to follow God's leading into dangerous times. There are also contemplative writers such as Kathleen Norris and Ruth Haley Barton who figure highly too. All of them begin their accounts with what is happening in their own life, and as they ponder where God is in it, they learn more about themselves. As they turn in gratitude to exploring a deepening relationship with this God, they share that with us too.

I notice that this list is all women. Not because there have not been male writers of significance to me. Of course, there have been. They predominate in books published, though perhaps not in the spiritual autobiography stream. But early on it was a growth step for me to affirm that women have something to offer *all* people, they do not write just for other women. So in valuing their example, I write for men as well.

This hesitation about women's experience being normative has its roots in another rejection. At a time when I had already published in several national magazines, I submitted an article to one of them, but for the first time, it drew specifically on my experience as a woman. The magazine

---

5. Benner, *Gift of Being Yourself,* 53.

rejected the material and returned it with the explanation that they did not have a woman's page! That very month however, they printed the account of a man's struggle with the guilt and forgiveness of his sin of visiting a prostitute. The magazine considered his story instructive for all readers, including women; a woman's story was apparently only instructive for women! I felt the shame of apparently being in an inferior class with nothing of value to offer the superior class. There are many things that God is changing in me through the transforming work of the Holy Spirit, but I have never expected it to include my gender! It reminds me that the early church had to learn that God did not require Gentiles to become Jews to be acceptable. And women do not need to be men to be loved by or serve God.

So *Finding Your voice: Engaging Confidently in All God Created You to Be* is an invitation to both women and men to discover and revel in how God wants you to live your life with all the good gifts given to you. Some of the issues discussed are more acute for women in *finding their voice* but my hope is that men will read those pages too in the spirit of #HeForShe. We all need people around us to encourage us. Men, there will be women around you—your wife, daughter, sister, friend, colleague, employee—who will appreciate your understanding and support.

A GIFT FOR MEN TOO

It is, in fact, a gift for men when the women around them can fully use their God-given gifts in the work sphere or the ministry they share, as well as in their families. Australian Annabel Crabb in her book, *The Wife Drought: Why Women Need Wives, and Men Need Lives,* humorously and comprehensively demonstrates from anecdotes and data that most fathers want more engagement with their children *plus* less pressure to perform in their paid work. They want a life! Possibilities open for men as well as women when the balance between their roles and workload is reassessed in a true sense of partnership.

Of course, finding your voice may also cause you to see that some doors should be firmly closed. I was trained in singing and enjoyed "performing" solos with my classical voice at 1960s youth rallies. It was a different era. I would not be welcome to do it now. I am old and unsteady of voice, and fortunately we have moved away from soloist prima donnas. In any case, my voice does not suit the style of contemporary worship music. Once when I was joining in the singing in a congregation, the person next to me asked what was wrong with my voice! Nothing wrong, just the wrong season for my kind of operatic voice. *Finding your voice* metaphorically can redirect you when you have pushed or wandered into the wrong arena of life and service. Or simply passed beyond that season of life. Being redirected can be as re-energizing as discovering your dream in the first place.

The journey to finding your voice begins with telling your story. As you hear your voice you will better understand how God has wired you. And your story will give you connection to others who can journey with you.

To encourage you to tell your story, I will recount a few of my own. That seems a very good place to start.

1

Start by Telling your Story

Words mean more than what is set down on paper. It takes the human voice to infuse them with shades of deeper meaning.
—Her teacher encouraging Maya Angelou to begin to speak.
(*I Know why the Caged Bird Sings*)

We all love a story. Stories entertain, they provide humor and laughter and perspective. They enliven a discussion and shift both the teller and the hearer from head down to the heart. They help us recognise our own pain and awaken empathy in us for others and pass on wisdom that connects us to the past and prepares us for the future. They may even prompt us to join important movements for change or become advocates for those who cannot speak for themselves. And they are a first step in the journey to *finding your voice*.

As I share some of my stories, I am hoping in them you will hear echoes of your own and find a way to tell yours. My life has come to feel like a pilgrimage directed by God's good hand, and I have learned a lot about myself and others as I travel it. You will too, if you take the time to look back, reflect, and identify God's footprints through your personal history.

A MISCARRIAGE STORY

One evening in the days when we lived in the United States and before we had children, we were hosting a dinner party for my husband's colleagues in our apartment. I was recovering from a miscarriage—the second one in the space of a year—and my mind kept turning to it over and over as I prepared the food. I did not know our dinner guests very well and besides, it was not usual to speak of personal matters in such a setting. Perhaps today it would be more acceptable, but certainly not in the 1970s. You did not talk about personal or sensitive things outside of friends and family, and even rarely with them. But for some reason, I mentioned the miscarriages as we sat around the dining table.

There was an embarrassed hush. Then several women in turn recounted their own pregnancy loss story and I realised for the first time how common miscarriage was. Each woman began her story by acknowledging that prior to this occasion, they had not told anyone outside their family about it. Clearly, the very hiddenness of the pregnancy loss had increased our pain because we had not been able to openly grieve it nor receive the release that comes from finding others who could enter personally into our distressing experience. In the presence of these women (and their husbands too), sharing my story was unexpectedly a gift to myself. It was a gift to them too, because healing comes through telling, hearing and sharing. How true it is that "there is no agony like bearing an untold story inside of you."[1]

SHARING WHAT WE HAVE IN COMMON

In the years since, I have experienced many groups sharing the story their members have in common. Sometimes, it has been as simple and expected as home group members describing their spiritual journey, but at other times, it has been a confronting, even risky thing to do.

In Canberra, the capital of Australia where we moved from the United States, a number of child sexual abuse survivors found each other and gathered in our church. They grouped themselves under the name of Tamar—the beautiful Old Testament woman, daughter of King David and sister of Absalom who was raped by her half-brother (2 Sam 13:1–29). These women found understanding and acceptance in each other. And even though many of our church members were reluctant to acknowledge the experience these

---

1. Maya Angelou and her autobiographical book, *I Know why the Caged Bird Sings* have long been credited with this observation. As appropriate as that would be, its source is unknown.

women shared, the Tamar women had the courage to talk about the issue more widely. The recent #MeToo movement has similarly provided an umbrella for women to identify with a growing sexual harassment awareness and tell their own story in a way most would not have dared to do, even a few years previously.

At that time in Canberra, we also began playgroups. In contrast to the Tamar sexual abuse survivor group, playgroups, though also a new phenomenon at the time, were readily appreciated and applauded. We embraced this innovative movement to give our pre-school children friends to play with because few of us in this newly built city had extended family nearby. The bonus was that the playgroups also provided a setting for young mothers to share stories of child-raising, and so learn from each other. Playgroups still do that today, though there are fathers and grandparents included now and a greater acknowledgement that they are valuable for both the children *and* the caregivers.

THE EMOTIONAL BONUS OF TELLING OUR STORY

It is great to hear others' stories, especially when they encourage us to share our own, but there is an even greater bonus that comes through the actual *act of telling*. Every story is unique and has meaning, but my own story is uniquely mine. Mine to tell. It comes with feelings, consequences, and perhaps explanations. You too have a story which is unique to you. It is rewarding to have a safe place to tell it and examine what it shows you about yourself, identifying what is most important to you. And it can open you to a new understanding of how God is leading you into the fullness of *finding your voice*.

The benefit that comes with *telling* our story operates at several levels. First is the biological reason: neuroscientists have demonstrated through their research that the active part of our brain associated with motivation and pleasure, lights up when we talk about what is happening in our life.[2] We are rewarded for talking about ourselves! The dopamine hit it gives us feels very good—a safe way of getting a high! No wonder the increased opportunities to do this through social media have become so popular.

Research shows that we experience this positive neural activity whether anyone hears us or not, but the satisfying effect is greatly enhanced if we share our thoughts and experiences with an empathetic listener. Presumably, this is God's design to encourage us to connect with others. We are

---

2. One example of this research is Ward, "The neuroscience of everyone's favorite topic."

made for relationships—it is how we are wired. Friendships, work settings, marriages, and communities are richer and deeper over time as we get to know one another through revealing ourselves. Communicating in these relationships goes to the core of what it means to be human. We build trust and connection by disclosing who we are in opening ourselves to another.

OUR STORIES HELP US UNDERSTAND OURSELVES

The second bonus of telling our story is the self-understanding it offers. Nancy Beach says, "As I listen to my life and tell my stories, a voice emerges."[3] This involves accepting who we are as a result of our family history and life experience. It includes becoming aware of what is going on for us in the present. And all is brought into focus by telling our story, hopefully to a great listener or two.

Early in my journey of finding my voice, I was surprised that whenever I read Jesus' story of the wedding guests needing suitable garments to wear, tears welled up. Strange. I came to see that it had something to do with the fact that my husband and I had been married in a foreign country with none of our family present. I had arranged the wedding myself, including quickly making my dress and that of the bridesmaid (whom I had only just met) in the limited time before the big day.

This was not an unfamiliar pattern, however. From the time I was a teenager, my mother had handed over to me all the important organizing tasks in the household. You do it better than me, she always said. For my coming-of-age twenty-first birthday party, this certainly applied. I did all the arrangements and my parents simply attended. Whether it was true or not, I came to feel deep down that I had not been adequately "mothered."

One day, at the retreat that was part of my doctoral course in California, I found a sympathetic listener and started to relate my story. I am not sure how much he said or what insights he provided, but in telling the story at his prompting, I began to see my mother's story. An ambitious young woman, she nevertheless had to leave school at fourteen to care for her sick mother. She found herself ill-equipped to run the household because up to that time they had live-in help, sometimes a maid, sometimes a maiden aunt. It was now thrust on her to manage the family home herself despite not being trained in housecraft either by her mother or one of these assistants. When I, her only daughter, was able to do what was needed, she handed it over to me. It was a kind of emotional co-dependency. She herself had a hunger to be mothered—not unexpected in the emotional absence of *her* mother.

---

3. Beach, *Gifted to Lead*, 123.

Someone has said that *understanding* is halfway to *forgiving*, and that was certainly what changed my attitude to my mother. But it was a major change towards myself as well. It was a step towards understanding who I was and how I functioned, facilitated by finding a good listener. God had more healing to do in this matter at the Californian retreat, but that is to tell later. Self-revealing was the first step then and still is—and it came through sharing my story.

THE GRANDMOTHERS OF ZIMBABWE

Others have tapped therapeutically into this power of telling a story. In Zimbabwe, a country greatly lacking support services for people experiencing mental distress, a psychiatrist developed an approach to bring services to the many throughout the country. Over the more than ten years since its inception, the successful program has come to be known by its two primary tools—the *friendship bench* and its *grandmothers*. Older women volunteers are recruited, given basic training in active listening and assessment skills, and an introduction to cognitive behaviour therapy. They are then sent out to sit on a bench in their local area with people needing a listening ear. The goal is to have a friendship bench within walking distance of every person in the country and a grandmother seated there with them.

These grandmothers do not offer advice, though they may share their lived experience. They listen sensitively as a friend, creating space for the person to describe their distress, helping them understand it better, and then be empowered by that process to resolve it themselves. Clearly, the first step of this problem-solving is to invite the person experiencing mental distress to tell their story in their mother tongue.

The results have been astounding in reducing depression and demands on medical and psychological services. As this grassroots mental health program has spread to other places and settings, including to New York City, men as well as women, and younger ones too, are serving as volunteer listeners. But the primary tool facilitating recovery of distressed people, remains the invitation to tell their story to an empathetic listener.

STORYTELLING IN MENTORING

I have been privileged to mentor many women and men who are discovering a flourishing new life in Jesus. Our conversations mostly focus on what God is doing here and now, but the backstory is important and usually where we start. I invite the person to tell me their story. Who are their parents and siblings? What have been the significant events in their life? Can they divide their life into its different seasons? When have they felt closest to God? To others? What dark times have they passed through? Can they name what came out of those times? Can they identify some recurring themes in how they live or how they hear God? Do some Bible stories resonate with them more than others?

Sometimes just having another hear their narrative is enough to move the person into a deeper spiritual journey. At other times as mentor, I can bring perspective into their situation so that they see the patterns of who they are and what God is doing in them at this season of their life. Then together we celebrate experiencing God's delight in the potential of their creation. Nothing gives me more joy than seeing a woman or a man unfurl into God's sunshine as the flourishing daughter or son the Creator intended from their beginning. The journey with their mentor may start with telling their story but it is an on-going story, and the person may have cause to return to it at other points in the relationship.

TELLING OUR STORY ENLARGES OUR UNDERSTANDING OF GOD

The third bonus of telling our story is that it enlarges our understanding of God. It becomes a way of opening-up our thinking about God as well as about our self. For fifteen years I wrote a quarterly column for the journal *Zadok Perspectives*. My husband and I were part of *Zadok*[4] almost from its beginnings in Canberra. It was created to encourage the application of biblical truth to everyday life in Australia at the intersection of Christianity and society. Most of my theological reflections birthed through those columns had their conception in the ordinary experiences and events of life and society around me—returning to Australia from overseas, the new phenomenon of computers, the surf and sand of Perth's beaches, once being caught in an ocean rip, city life, and later, letting go of our children. I benefited from telling my story to what proved to be a sympathetic audience and it deepened my understanding of both Scripture and life, especially of the nature of God's work in me. Some of the fruit of those reflections is found in the pages of this book.

This God is the prime mover in your life too. Examining your experience and where the Holy Spirit has been active is important. Listening to

---

4. *Zadok* is now part of *Ethos: Evangelical Alliance Centre for Christianity and Society* headquartered in Melbourne, Australia.

your life with a companion, through a journal or in private contemplation, is a simple step along the way to *finding your voice*.

TRUE HUMILITY

There is, however, an issue I must address in encouraging you to tell your story. It is the accusation that to talk about yourself, to focus on your experiences or your heart's desires, is being too self-centered. Some claim it is the opposite of godly humility. Pride is, of course, a danger if we take credit for what we have achieved or the difficulties we have overcome. But true humility does not deny the good in our lives. Rather, it acknowledges that everything we have comes in grace from the hand of the Creator.

The remedy for pride is found in *using* what we have been given to serve God and others. "Blessed to be a blessing," my daughter-in-law has written on her whiteboard to remind herself of her primary motivation in helping others. That is what demonstrates true humility. In the next chapter, we will look at how God gives both creation and spiritual gifts to equip us to serve. If we dismiss or neglect who we are created to be, that is as God-denying as taking pride in our personal accomplishments. Unfortunately, sometimes out of fear or false humility we pull back from appreciating our potential. This is damaging to ourselves as well as to God's work in the world.

There is an even more compelling reason for telling our story, however, and an impetus for examining and revealing ourselves. It is that we are made in the image of the self-revealing Creator. The Scriptures, starting from Genesis and reaching their fulfilment in the coming of Jesus, are a gradual unveiling of the nature of the three-in-one God—the relationship God.

GOD TELLS US HIS STORY

My husband and I have always enjoyed building friendships through small groups wherever we have lived. Often these have been in the church we were part of and centred on the Scriptures. Together with the other group members we have sought to find God's wisdom for living in a rapidly changing society and contemporary culture. And time and time again, the new insights and perspectives we have needed, have come as people have told stories of their experience of God's work in their lives.

A few years ago, I noticed that when older people joined our groups it took some time for them to be comfortable with the personal sharing this approach encourages. Truth for previous generations was often thought of as abstract doctrines, expressed in tones of black and white, rather than through story. Much has shifted! Today our speaking of God may perhaps feel more nebulous and less authoritative, yet stories have proven to be the best way to encourage each other to grow in God and follow Jesus in our world. That is not surprising, because story is God's own chosen method of communicating with us through the Scriptures.

These biblical God stories are often great yarns, full of humor and incidental details that paint a vivid picture of life then and there. Entertaining and memorable narratives are the way societies usually pass on their culture and traditional values to the next generation, but biblical stories are more than moral lessons, even though the wisdom of the ages is enshrined in them. Their primary purpose is to tell us what God is doing in this world—a world created in all its complexity and beauty but now infected with pain. In particular, they tell us that our Creator wants to relate to us, to talk to us about our self, and remind us how we are created to respond to the divine acts of love. The God-stories are about relationship.

I have seen that my colleagues in East Africa whose families and congregations are pressured by poverty, frequently use tales of Old Testament heroes in their preaching to inspire their congregations in the knowledge that God has not forgotten them. Hebrew leaders and prophets did the same, often in language and pictures coming to them as the *word of the Lord*. In each of their stories the important thing is that God is the hero, keeping promises in the messy lives of people and leaders who sometimes follow, sometimes wander away, but are still loved.

JESUS' LIFE IN STORIES

The New Testament also contains great stories. There are no better examples than those from Jesus' life, including the stories he himself told. Who has not been confronted by the parable of the good Samaritan or the picture of the boss who pays all his workers above and beyond the agreed rate whether they have earned it or not, or the bridesmaids who miss out on the wedding because they are not ready for the bridegroom's arrival. Jesus' stories, resonating with local references to everyday life, reveal wisdom in unexpected ways that push us out of our neat systems of understanding, and help us recognise, not just truth, but his heart. When challenged about his identity and purpose, Jesus pointed to both his actions and to his often-surprising teaching—much of it presented through stories. More memorable than abstract doctrine, his teaching is the lens through which all doctrine must be filtered.

Unfortunately, we sometimes treat these Jesus narratives as belonging in children's Sunday School while we mature people have "graduated" to learning the Christian faith through the more systematic theology of letters written by the Apostle Paul and other first-century leaders. As a result, we do not read the four gospels as often as they warrant, or read one gospel right through, like a gripping story. We know how the story ends and so miss the suspense leading to the tragedy of Jesus' cross, or we fail to feel how devastating to their hopes his death was for his followers. They had no expectation of his coming to life again. Similarly, we can hardly appreciate their overflowing joy at being reunited with their Master. Yet personally experiencing the resurrected Jesus, was what propelled his followers to risk death to share the good news of his saving love across a hostile world. And they did that by telling his story.

THIS SELF-REVEALING GOD

The most important biblical encouragement for us to tell our story, however, is that both the Old and New Testament describe a God who takes the initiative in self-revealing, showing us the way. We are invited by psalmists and prophets to know and respond, not just to a Creator, but to a loving and faithful shepherd, a redeemer, a husband—to name just a few of the relationship metaphors used to emphasise the welcoming care of this God who goes to great lengths to offer us forgiveness and deep bonding. A God of power and the glory, yes, but also of great patience and love. And again and again, God's loving nature is uncovered through story.

Even the Old Testament prophets known for thundering against evil, told stories. They were illustrating God's faithful *hesed*, as well as wrath. This very rich Hebrew word means unwavering lovingkindness and mercy. It describes God's attitude even to errant people who continually fail and ignore their obligations. At my father's funeral, several of his former students told me *hesed* was one of his favorite biblical words. Whenever he spoke of it in lectures, and that was frequently, they noticed his eyes would twinkle and his smile widen as he waxed lyrical about the loving way God treats us.[5] I like to think those twinkling eyes and widening smile are just a little glimpse of God's face, revealed to us in Scripture.

Then into human history, Jesus comes—the supreme revealing of the divine nature. His disciples once asked Jesus how they could know the holy God he spoke about, so he gave them glimpses of his relationship with the Father—*his* Father. Later when they received the Holy Spirit, the unveiling

---

5. Some of Ted Gibson's teaching on *hesed* is reproduced in Ingram, *Glimpses of Glory*.

of God as three-in-one completed a circle of love and relationship in a way never fully seen before.

This self-revealing God is the one in whose image we are created. We too are to be self-revealing because relationship is central to our being. We are most fully human when connected to others and we cannot relate deeply if we withhold our true self. So when we resist carefully sharing our story with others because it feels self-centered or embarrassing, we must remind ourselves: you were made for this, you are made like the self-revealing God.

BUILDING RELATIONSHIPS THROUGH REVEALING OUR SELF

Disclosing our self is how others come to know us. It is how we build connection and we have probably all observed how it works. Growing a relationship with a person moves like a measured step by step dance towards the other. Starting far apart, we approach the person emotionally, but if one of us moves forward too quickly physically or relationally, we instinctively take a step back, because revealing too much, too soon and without appropriate preparation, makes us retreat. Rather, if we say a little that is personal and the other responds in kind, we feel free to move towards them some more. In their further response, we then find courage for the next step of self-revealing, as we gently step towards each other.

People sometimes dismiss as having no value the simple chit-chat or exchange of careful non-identifying information at the beginning of a conversation. But it is, in fact, testing the waters. Is this person open? Are they accepting of me? Can we move safely towards each other at a measured pace? The twenty-first century desire to accelerate this getting-to-know-you process by speed dating, for example, or through a Tinder app, can cause great hurt in intimate relationships. But the promise and the danger apply in other relationships too. I have occasionally seen someone come into a small group and, hungry to share their story, tell too much on a first occasion. "Spilling their guts," we call it, or "over-sharing." They usually do not come again to the group—out of embarrassment perhaps, but also because they think wrongly that this cluster of people is not accepting of them. Rather, it was just too much too soon.

HEARING ANOTHER PERSON'S STORY—THE GIFT OF EMPATHY

Hearing another's story is also a gift. We get a glimpse of what it is like to walk in their shoes. It may grow our understanding and empathy in a scenario we have never personally encountered. In fact, we may not even be aware of how ignorant we are regarding this scenario. There is, of course, no substitute for lived experience, but gaining understanding through someone who has been there, can open our eyes. And when we connect to the storyteller and feel their emotion, we cannot easily turn away from them.

In our years living in urban America, our white church wrestled with its connection to the neighboring public housing area. A nearby black church invited us to spend a weekend living in the slum with members of their congregation. To take up the offer was a form of tokenism on our part, I suppose, but it did help us go some way to understanding and connecting with our hosts as we heard from them the consequences of being black and confined to a "black" area of the city. It was tokenism, because it did not change the way most of us continued to live and conduct church in our more privileged area. However, it did later inform my work as a town planning consultant. In assessing a scheme to provide housing for residents from nearby New York City, for example, I recognised the inherent discrimination in what was proposed. I saw it through the faces of real people I had met that weekend in our own city.

STORIES FROM AFRICA

In more recent years, my colleagues and students in East Africa have added depth to my understanding of the daily struggle of living in poverty. Abandoned wives and widows have told me their stories of isolation and lack of food, but they usually name their greatest challenge finding school fees so their children can finish high school. They desperately hope education will save their young people from being trapped in generational poverty like their own. They hold this hope even when many students cannot find a job even when they graduate. The centrality of this hope—that the future will be better than the past—has influenced my teaching and motivated our team to respond in more specific and appropriate ways.

It has also shown me how little I know about living with trauma. The stories from people living with the impact of HIV Aids have been the most confronting. In the final session of a workshop I recently conducted in Uganda, the pastors and leaders were discussing the very challenging biblical call to forgive an aggressor. One woman shared her story. Her husband had abandoned her and the family some years before and left the village. But in his life of new freedoms, he contracted HIV Aids and became increasingly ill. Finally, he came home, desperately demanding not only that his wife care for him, but that she also welcome him back into her bed. What did forgiving involve for her? The discussion that followed I could never have prompted as an outsider to their culture. It will forever deepen my empathy for people who have so much to forgive. And in the future, I will talk less and leave more space for them to tell their stories.

EARTHQUAKE IN KATHMANDU

In April 2015, my husband and I found ourselves in the center of a major disaster. We were in Kathmandu, the capital of Nepal, at the time of the earthquake. Frightened, unsure what to do and not aware at first of how severe the damage was or how badly the locals were affected, we finally managed to return to our hotel, and camped out in the grounds for several days.

Who lived, who died in the earthquake seemed quite random. Our hotel building was largely intact though a nearby one completely collapsed into its basement, killing all those inside. We slept in our clothes with only intermittent electricity and bailed water for the toilet. The continuing and unsettling threat of aftershocks dominated our days. Every tremor made us afraid again. It was even more so for poorly resourced Nepalese. Police and other rescuers were few and people milled around in the streets, staying away from other buildings threatening to collapse and camping out in any open space. It was a sobering experience to see them abandoned while we felt helpless to do anything constructive to assist.

By the third day, we ventured to eat inside the hotel dining room once more but kept rushing out whenever the table or the overhead light started shaking. The hotel was largely out of food by then anyway. Some other foreigners (the guards remaining at the gate only admitted foreigners) took shelter with us because their hotels had collapsed or were locked up by the owner. The number of people waiting, waiting, waiting, increased.

Of course, we rich westerners were better off than most. We had food for those few days, though no staff to cook it for us—they had all gone home to look for their families. We just raided the kitchen till it ran out. Meanwhile, local shops serving the city residents had shut straight away and all food distribution stopped.

When the airport finally opened, we were instructed to take the first opportunity to fly out. Tourists were in the way and not helpful to rescue efforts. This meant joining the massive crush around abandoned check-in desks, trying to get information about our flight. We were in effect, desperate if temporary refugees, elbowing our way in, scrambling for what little was available and pushing past others to get it. I was embarrassed to find myself in that stampede. I carry survivor guilt that we left when others could not. This was reinforced by the clapping that broke out in the plane as we made our escape—we were the fortunate ones. Nevertheless, I gained some understanding of what it means to be a refugee and can view those in more straightened circumstances with less condemnation for the "illegal" efforts they make to support their family.

MATCHING STORIES

We have told the Kathmandu story many times, of course. From years of hiking and camping, even once losing a canoe in rapids from under our youngest son, we have a saying in our family that the *worst* experiences make the *best* stories. Nevertheless, our "Kathmandu in an earthquake" is a tourist's story—an exceptional one, granted, but the kind that when you tell it, others match it with one of their own. We have since been told of countless other earthquakes, including an extremely rare one in our part of Australia back in 1968! The acceptable reason for this matching of stories is that when someone tells you their trauma story, you show that you understand at least a little what they have experienced by telling one of your own. You are assuring them of your empathy while enjoying connecting through a facet of your life that you have in common.

But there is an unworthy reason for matching stories too and most of us have experienced the pain of that. As we tell our story, the person hearing it is tempted to go one better—swamping our story with their own and proving they are superior adventurers or perhaps braver survivors. Even tales of adversity can be used to outdo another person's! So when someone opens up with their story, the listener must hold back, because coming in fast with an equivalent tale belittles the teller's and does not leave space to hear the emotion behind their words or give due weight to its significance. We all need someone to hear our story, reflect on it with us, perhaps carefully add some insights on what it signifies, but above all, listen with empathy and resist the temptation to launch into one of our own. I know I have been guilty of that on occasion.

Even someone who is not naturally an empathetic listener can learn the skill of attentive listening and practice it. They can stop talking, ask only appropriate questions, not be too ready to add their own thoughts, and let the person choose their own pace for self-revealing.

START TELLING YOUR STORY

Good friends give each other this gift of listening but we can also seek out a safe place to be heard through an intentional relationship offered by a trained mentor or counsellor. If you have never had the opportunity to be listened to deeply, this is a good first step in your journey of self-discovery. Locate someone who will listen to your story with empathy and insight as you begin to see who God has created you to be and where your life's journey is taking you. Your story opens your past to you as well as your present. It gives you words to express what you have experienced and felt and thought and where you are now. It helps you see the imprint of God in your life as you continue your pilgrimage, because you are not alone. Take courage to begin the conversation with God and others as you learn to listen to your life.

Personal Reflection

Has someone given you the benefit of listening to your story? Were you comfortable in talking about yourself in this way? If not, can you identify why it was difficult for you?

As you told your story, what aspects of your life did you realise for the first time were significant for you? How will you process this discovery?

If you have not yet discovered an empathetic listener or mentor, you may find putting your life story down on paper helpful. Make sure you include the period before you were aware of a personal relationship with God, because the Creator was vitally interested in you then as well.

Writing your spiritual autobiography can draw attention to themes that you have not noticed before. As you briefly describe the significant events and dramas of your life with its ups and the downs, identify the footprints of God in it. Perhaps you can choose one theme to explore further.

2

Listen to Your Life

Listen to your life; pay attention to what happens to you . . . If God is really involved with the world, then one of the most powerful ways God speaks to us is through what happens to us, which means keep your ears open, keep your eyes open for the often hidden, elusive word of God.

—Frederick Buechner (*Whistling in the Dark*)

When you start by telling your story, you are listening to your past, your family heritage, the culture you were born into. The next step in *finding your voice* is to move into the present and see what God is doing now in all the ups and downs of your current life. I encourage you to *listen to your life* for, as Buechner says, this is one of the most powerful ways God speaks to us.

HUMBLE, COMPASSIONATE, AND ADAPTABLE BARNABAS

One of my favorite Bible characters who listened to his life is Barnabas—a godly man "full of the Holy Spirit and faith." We first meet him in the early days of the church when he generously sells some land and gives the proceeds to the poverty-stricken Christians in Jerusalem (Acts 4:36–37). This and his subsequent actions show him to be a man of great compassion and empathy. Twice he sponsors the young Saul, the vigorous persecutor of the

Christians, after his professed conversion to Jesus on the road to Damascus. Others are still frightened of Saul and doubt his sincerity, thinking this may be a ruse to get inside the Christian community and continue to imprison and kill them. But Barnabas listens to him and is convinced of the reality of his spiritual turn-around. He goes out of his way to support him in a meeting with the apostles in Jerusalem.

Later Barnabas is commissioned by those leaders to investigate what is stirring in the distant Syrian Antioch church, where surprisingly, non-Jews in great numbers are becoming Christians. He travels there and concludes that this too is the work of God, creating a new frontier for the gospel. So he looks for Saul to apprentice him in ministry and invite him to help nurture these new Christians. He finds him back in his hometown in Turkey and brings him to Antioch to team-teach with him. The new Gentile converts in Antioch come from cultures without the Old Testament background to readily understand Jesus and his teaching. Barnabas, having grown up outside Palestine, is the person to bridge the gap to these new Christians and he recognises that this applies as well to Saul with his Greek education. He will be an ideal protégé alongside him in this new center of the Christian church.

When at a later date, the now-established Antioch church decides to send out these two teachers under Barnabas' leadership to take the gospel to a more northernly Roman province, a startling reversal of their roles soon becomes evident. Saul, now using his Greek name, Paul, becomes the recognised leader and Barnabas takes a back seat (Acts 13:13; 14:12).

BARNABAS RESPONDS WELL TO THIS REVERSAL OF ROLES

I have often wondered how he felt about his relegation to second position, but apparently it had become clear to Barnabas as the journey progressed, that Paul with his energetic type A personality should set the pace. Probably the younger man's impeccable background in the Hebrew, Greek, and Roman cultures, gifts of oratory and theological and philosophical thinking, have already made him the more prominent figure. So Barnabas, the insightful and gentle sponsor of young leaders, is prepared to make way for his protégé. It is a wonderful example of someone knowing himself and his gifting and acting within it as he saw what God was doing in his (and Paul's) life. It enables him to team with a dominant character like Paul, even as Paul becomes the center of the New Testament narrative through the writings of his biographer Luke. Eventually Barnabas and Paul part ways over the older man's support for the errant John Mark, but in this also, he was later proved correct in continuing to support the young man's future, just as he was in his earlier support of Paul.

Barnabas knew himself and the situation in which he found himself. Similarly, knowing yourself by listening to your life, will equip you to see where you fit into God's plans for his world. It will give you the courage to tread difficult paths, even to reassess where you are going and change in mid-life. You can aspire to be as bold and adaptable as Barnabas.

WHAT DID GOD HAVE IN MIND FOR YOU AT YOUR CREATION?

Most of us long for the confidence and settled security of knowing who God has made us to be. Traditionally this is known as discovering your vocation or call, but it is not necessarily a call to Christian ministry as usually understood. That is why I am using the expression, *finding your voice,* because you may be called to use that voice in leadership in the general community rather than the church community. Or perhaps through your profession, your home or some other sphere of service or activity.

In the church I am now part of, we talk about serving God "in your place of access"—the place where you have entry—such as school or workplace or sporting club. At the beginning of each year, we recognise and pray publicly for people in each category of *place of access*—education, business, sports field, the home front, and so on. We acknowledge each of us is God's person in that place and we want as a church community, to support each other in it. For most people, their place of access is outside the gathered church, not within it.

Lloyd John Ogilvie, chaplain to the Senate of the United States in the 1990s and renowned preacher, was reported to have asked in a sermon, "What difference would it make in your life if you could see what God had in mind when he created you?" That is a good question, but it does not have a simple answer because it is designed rather to cause us to reflect on what we know about our *self* and to ponder the potential we see there as part of God's design. The important thing about our *voice* is that it comes from God—it has the Creator's imprimatur.

Discovering your voice involves asking questions and listening to your life as you interpret the finger of God active in it. You may have begun attending to God's promptings tentatively in your teenage years but with experience you have grown in your ability to hear and understand them. You may also have come to see what you are *not* called to, as well as what you are. You may have tried several avenues of work or service before finding what best fits with who you are at this stage of your life. But even when the nuances of your call evolve over time and the locations where you live it out change, there is usually a lifelong thread which is uniquely yours because it is how God has made you—your spiritual/emotional DNA.

THE FIRST QUESTION—WHAT GIVES YOU JOY?

In encouraging us to examine our life, Buechner has observed, "The place God calls you to is the place where your deep gladness and the world's deep hunger meet."[1] This suggests two questions to ask yourself as you listen to your life. Firstly, what in your life of service gives you joy?

If you are used to thinking that following Jesus only means taking up your cross, this focus on personal joy, on fulfilment, may come as a surprise. Joy? In serving? Isn't being a disciple simply hard self-sacrificing work? But if *how* you serve is in line with *how* God has wired you, why should it not give you joy? You are created in the image of the God who, Genesis 1 tells us, looked at what was made, and after each creative day's work, pronounced it *good*. The seventh day of creation, the day marking its completion, became the rest of satisfaction, God enjoying *all* that was created. Someone has described the created world as God's cathedral—not just a high-vaulted building, but something far grander, giving its Creator great delight. The vast wonders of nature—sunsets, storms, mountains, forest, ocean—provoke awe in us. That God enjoys these too is marvellous, even more so when we remember that the peak of God's creation was not the grand natural world, but the man and the woman—made like God for creativity and relationship.

Whatever we do to create—cook, paint, sew, speak, write, garden, put together a car, or code some new software—we are intended to get a high in the doing of it. Joy! Just like our God did at creation. By noticing in yourself what most gives you this satisfaction, you have a strong pointer to how God has created you to contribute to this world. Certainly that includes, but is not limited to, the creative arts. Most creative activities are difficult and require patient discipline, but they are more than worth the effort for the joy they bring.

Do you talk with others about your satisfaction in creating? Are you able to put into words what you enjoy? Like many of the aspects of life we are considering in these pages, naming your source of joy can feel as if you are boasting. But if you acknowledge it all comes from your Creator and express your gratitude for this gracious gift, it will enable you to expand into all you are meant to be, to *finding your voice*.

---

1. Buechner, *Listening to your Life*, 186.

It is said that of all pursuits, speaking in front of others in a formal setting is the most anxiety-producing activity possible. Yet if that is what you are created to do, it should bring you satisfaction as well as anxiety. I have noticed that people just starting out preaching or public speaking, are often wary of acknowledging they get joy out of doing it. Of course, it requires humility, and it feels like a heavy weight of responsibility. After twenty minutes or so of speaking, you may spend the next hour (or week) agonizing over how you could have done it better. But does it give you pleasure? If so, then it may be a piece of what God has made you for. The same applies to any activity you undertake that requires creativity and is purposefully assisting people. There are many other factors to take into account in listening to God's call, but noticing this joy is a good starting point.

For myself, the greatest joy comes from learning something new and then sharing it with others. This applied when I initially trained as a teacher, then as I practiced as a town planner, and later, in mid-life when I began preaching. It shapes many of my conversations with people I mentor, even with my grandchildren. I love taking the deep things of God from the world and the Scriptures and trying to put them in terms others can grasp and live by. Perhaps that is the main motivation behind this book!

It is not easy to acknowledge our source of joy. It sounds like pride in our own accomplishments. I found it helpful the first time I tried to put it in words, to do it with my mentor, and more recently, with others who share a similar aspiration. I continue to discover a more nuanced understanding of what gives me joy as time goes by.

THE SECOND QUESTION—WHERE DO YOU SEE DEEP HUNGER?

Buechner's second question to ask is: Where do you see the world's *deep hunger*? Do you burn with indignation when you discover injustice? Are you impatient to put it right? Maybe you have learned to use that indignation to motivate you to loud and urgent action. You want to shout, "How dare you!" J. I. Packer says of God's anger that it is "a right and necessary reaction to moral evil."[2] You may have been wired to have more of that godly response to wrongdoing or exploitation than other people. In fact, others' indifference to evil may be particularly galling to you. Injustice then is your place of seeing the world's deep hunger.

Or maybe you have great empathy for someone who is suffering, and quietly step in to walk alongside them. You feel with them and appreciate

---

2. Packer, *Knowing God*, 151.

what their situation is costing them and how it is handicapping them. Or when you see a lonely person, you find it the most natural thing to offer simple hospitality without taking over their life or being paternalistic. These are all indications of where your place of ministry should be, or perhaps already is.

Some of us respond at a very individual or personal level, working one-on-one with people. Others are concerned about the societal or community structures that cause or facilitate evil. Ask yourself if seeing something wrong behind the scenes or noticing a neglected procedure, stirs you to action. Are you concerned about fixing these problems before they damage the underlying operation of a community or a school or a church or society as a whole? Do you take a risk to draw attention to the deficiency, and become a whistle-blower? Or begin a protest movement? Listening to your life includes noticing the things that move and motivate you to action, even as you appreciate that not everyone sees or responds in the same way. Our compassion or concern expresses itself in different patterns. We are all wired differently, and we become aware of that "wiring" when we listen and observe our reactions.

In the volatile nineteen-sixties and seventies when we were living in the United States, our group of friends engaged actively with the social issues of the day in our city, but we responded in varied ways. A few campaigned on the streets for human rights. At the time the Black Panther trials were moved nearby from California and some of our friends joined the demonstrations, while others were in the basement of the church making sandwiches and providing a sanctuary for tear-gassed protestors. One wrote a book calling on Christians to see the hunger around them and do something about it. Others housed ghetto teenagers during the week in their suburban homes so the students could go to a better high school. Some tutored students still trapped in the poorer city schools.

My husband and I did not engage in the street protests, but we were part of a regular group discussion among graduate students which we called *Areopagus*. It was named after the place of public discourse in ancient Athens where the Apostle Paul engaged with local thinkers after observing their altar to the unknown God. Our group was created to encourage these young PhD students, the cream of American academia at the beginning of their professional lives, to engage as Christians with public issues, sharing their insights across disciplines. Many of those who joined with us in *Areopagus* have later contributed significantly through their writing and teaching to Christian thought in the United States and wider afield. At the time I was practicing as a town planner and this started my thinking "christianly" about my professional planning work.

THE NEEDS WE SEE MAY CHANGE OVER TIME

My husband was clear from his teenage years that agriculture would be in his future. Supplying food for the world's hungry people has been his motivation for a lifetime of scientific endeavour. He has made a significant contribution to improving yields in rain-fed crop production through expanding scientists' understanding of how plants work. Observing growing things and their condition is his daily practice. He notices weeds, for example. Where we now live is close to the Indian Ocean. In recent years, the conservation group of which he was a member made a concerted effort to replant the foreshore with native species to stabilize the cliffs and sand dunes. We walk down regularly to the foreshore to check how the plants are surviving without irrigation in our hot Western Australian summer. And the agriculturalist always sees and pulls weeds!

In contrast to my husband's steady trajectory, I have had a changing path. What began as a desire to understand, not plants, but society systems and the physical environments underpinning them, steered me into town planning. In the early days in the United States, this included consulting with local communities and writing books about septic systems and subdivisions, but later my focus was wetlands and other regional issues. Following our *Areopagus* experience, when we returned to Australia it was a short step to write about town planning from a theological perspective. Later that broadened to thinking and writing more generally on the theology of everyday life.

A desire to serve God through our professional work is what my husband and I have in common. We assert strongly that the Creator is interested in the physical wellbeing of people, as well as in their spiritual relationships. God wants us to understand, as best we can, how the created world is intended to function and invites us to join in using that knowledge to make people's lives better. Even though we human descendants of Adam and Eve mess up our world and treat people badly, we are still welcomed to participate in God's continuing work of redeeming and maintaining it.

My husband ranks curiosity as the most important characteristic for understanding and contributing to God's world. He constantly asks questions about how plants work to find ways to produce more food. I work with people asking parallel questions—how can we best live? I look at society, trying to understand the movements of ideas and ways of living. I ask what the Scriptures teach us about ourselves and our culture. My passion to explore Scripture and apply its principles to everyday life has flowed into the writing and teaching I have done over many years.

THE INTERSECTION—THE SWEET SPOT—
THE PLACE TO FIND YOUR VOICE

The intersection of the unique way God has made each one of us, and the needs we perceive and respond to most enthusiastically, is our sweet spot. This is the place where joy and personal fulfilment unite in serving others. Influenced by opportunity and our stage of life, it may seem vastly different in mature adulthood or retirement from our youthful passions, yet there will be elements of continuity linked to our personality and way of seeing the world.

In midlife, the pursuit of the sweet spot helped me change direction and realise that God was calling me to train as a pastor. I was already studying theology to gain a solid knowledge of the Bible to undergird my writing. I expected that my passion to relate the Scriptures to everyday life for ordinary Christians, would continue to be expressed primarily in my quarterly *Zadok* column and the training workshops I was conducting through the Australian Small Group Network. Then I noticed that each Sunday after church I was having substantial conversations with different people, and that many of these conversations were pastoral interactions. This greatly surprised me as I had not thought of myself as particularly having pastoral gifts, but I was listening to my life.

Meanwhile, I was also finding satisfaction through membership of several national and state-wide committees and realizing the value of the experience I had gained in consulting work in American and Australian towns as a planning professional. I started to see that through this earlier professional work, God had been preparing me also for church leadership. In my denomination, there were at that time very few women seeking pastoral roles, and those aspiring to it, though usually in their 30s or 40s, previously had been excluded from apprenticeship roles in church governance. They were coming to the role of pastor without whole-congregation leadership experience or any of the mentoring that established leaders usually offer to promising young men. Some had ceased working outside the home in their child-raising years and so had not benefitted from significant engagement in senior management in secular fields either.

I now saw the benefit of those distressing years of not having children after we married. They gave me seven years in America of stretching experience, working with municipal boards, addressing public meetings, and preparing public-friendly reports on substantive issues. I loved that work and left it only reluctantly, but I came to see the parallels to the church work God was now calling me to.

Janet Woodlock, in discussing women hearing God's call, observes that there is "something compelling about a clear and mature sense of Christian vocation: a conviction that 'I was created for this purpose.'"[3] But she goes on to add that if a culture does not support the direction the person feels called to follow, it can discourage them from seeking to discover their vocation. This is clearly true for many women. They may believe they are called to a role in society or the church, but it is not one open to them. This applied to me. It was a major challenge for me to own that God was calling me to pastoring when my denomination had no women pastors in my part of the world.

Not only women may be discouraged by societal expectations, however. Woodlock quotes Parker J. Palmer applying this hurdle more widely, and lamenting "we are trained away from true self toward images of acceptability; under social pressures like racism and sexism our original shape is deformed beyond recognition; and we ourselves, driven by fear, too often betray our true self to gain the approval of others."[4] This pressure to hide who we truly are, leads to what has been called the "imposter syndrome." We will address this in a later chapter. Women in particular fall into this predicament.

USING PERSONALITY PROFILES TO IDENTIFY YOUR SWEET SPOT

Listening to your life produces a growing self-understanding. But there are many additional tools you can also use to explore your developing abilities and preferences. The term *creation gifts*[5] is a useful way to describe these natural talents and personality characteristics that God has given. To give due weight to creation gifts, we must firstly distinguish them from *spiritual gifts*. We will look later at spiritual gifts, but it is important to first consider the ones that come from our natural heritage and upbringing.

Researchers do not agree to what extent these creation gifts are inherited. Are they solely the result of the parents' genes or are they due to the kind of nurturing environment the family provided? I have found that when people have their own children, they change their thinking about this and move closer to deciding that many tendencies are simply inborn! A stubborn child was born a stubborn child, for example! You cannot blame the parent or the home they provide for that! However, recent studies have

---

3. Woodlock, "Vocational Discernment," 9.
4. Woodlock, "Vocational Discernment," 10.
5. Adopted by Mulholland and Barton, *Invitation to a Journey*.

shown that the physical and psychological conditions in which a child is raised can change the child's inheritable traits, indicating that the interplay between our physical makeup and our environment is much more complex and malleable than once thought.

Our focus here, however, is on the personal characteristics and abilities we have already received. To help understand our personality and its strengths and challenges, there are various classifications. One of the best known is the Myers-Briggs[6] Type Indicator, and it has been used by many people to identify their creation gifts, particularly to understand how they work best with others in a team (or a marriage). It is based on Carl Jung's recognition of four pairs of essential but contrasting preferences common to everyone. Through a multiple question test you choose responses that are then classified as either extroversion (E) or introversion (I); intuition (N) or sensing (S); thinking (T) or feeling (F); and judgment (J) or perception (P). This gives one of sixteen possible combinations of personality types expressed in a four-letter code. But even within these sixteen types, people show many differences and variations in the strength of their preferences. That we can all be so different from one another reminds us that in our work or church or family, we will almost certainly approach life and relationships in a quite different way from those we are interacting with.

NO HIERARCHY OF CREATION GIFTS

Whatever classification system is used, and they are many others of varying complexity, the important point is that all types of personality are part of God's creation kaleidoscope and are to be valued. Each has its opportunities and responsibilities. There is no right or wrong personality, even though some people improperly use their strengths to exploit or damage others, rather than work together with them.

I have seen people have a great "Aha!" moment exploring their creation gifts for the first time. After years of devaluing their personality in comparison with some ideal, they recognise themselves in one of the many described types and have a new appreciation for their own personal value.

Especially when it comes to leadership, we often have in mind a hierarchy of personalities. Depending on the system being used, we may expect the classic leader to be a Myers-Briggs ENTJ or a *Type A* or a *Driver* or a *bull* or a choleric *lion*. A leader may be thought of as a vigorous extrovert, or a

---

6. Mulholland and Barton provide a good summary of the Jungian background and value of Myers-Briggs types in chapter 5, "Creation Gifts." Questionnaires are also available online.

hare spectacularly racing to the finish line. But in reality, the slow and steady tortoise, the quiet introvert, can get there first, or at least be more effective in leadership, bringing out the best in those around them. This is the message of Brian Harris' book, *The tortoise usually wins*. It would be exhausting if we were all hares—there is a place for tortoises too!

Personality classifications have a cultural dimension as well. What we value and how we describe each category varies greatly. This was brought home to me rather humorously in Kenya. I was explaining the behavior types with the animals used in western countries to illustrate degrees of assertiveness in five interpersonal styles—compelling bull, avoiding tortoise, compromising fox, accommodating dog, and collaborating owl. The students quickly pointed out that in their culture, a dog is not *accommodating*. Dogs are largely untamed, allowed to roam freely and ignore people—they are not pets. I jokingly suggested a koala instead to illustrate the cultural context of these symbols, but the Australian koala had no meaning for them.

However, their reaction to the collaborating owl was what most surprised me. Surely everyone thinks of the owl as a symbol of serene and considered wisdom, but I discovered that in Kenya its presence is considered a sign of evil. Who would want to have an owl personality? The participants suggested instead using a sheep as the symbol of collaboration. To an Australian, that was equally a surprise. We think of sheep, and especially a mob of sheep, as quite unruly and difficult to handle, requiring a well-trained sheepdog or two. Certainly not wise or collaborative. I later realised my students were probably thinking of how sensible and cooperative a sheep is compared with the irrepressible goats they run together with them. It was a reminder that how we describe our creation gifts must be in the context of our community and through listening to others' observations. Creation gifts are not just individual traits for us to use how we will, but for us to live and work together.

DO OUR CREATION GIFTS CHANGE?

Classification systems are an inexact attempt to organise complex reality. So in real life we should not think personality types put us in an iron-clad box, but there is usually a general continuity through our life from our childhood. However, as Christians, we also know that the Holy Spirit is working in us to make us more like Christ. That suggests some modification or change in emphasis in our personality is possible—perhaps a softening or removal of "sharp corners" or giving attention to dysfunctional habits that should change.

This is one of the values of the Enneagram.[7] This ancient system invites a person to identify which basic *human need* is most characteristic of them. The word enneagram comes from the Greek word for nine and the nine *needs* identified in this classification are the *need*—to be perfect; to be loved and needed; to be successful; to be special; to have knowledge and fulfilment; to be secure; to avoid pain; to have power; or to attain emotional peace. Through a self-assessment questionnaire or the assistance of someone trained in the schema, you identify which one of those nine needs resonates most strongly with your motivations and ways of viewing and interacting with the world. The resources associated with the Enneagram then provide you with a direction for letting God's Spirit address the human temptation in you to be self-sufficient and meet this need in yourself, rather than in God. There is a built-in expectation that as you uncover the hurtful tendencies and needs in your personality, you can grow in godliness. I recommend it as a tool to listen to your life and nurture your relationship with God.

KNOWING WHAT DOES NOT GIVE YOU JOY

A further nuance to thinking about what gives deep gladness was apparent in a phone conversation I had recently. The young woman was asking advice on whether she should accept a job she had been offered which seemed to fit her skills and experience very appropriately. As she described the employment conditions and the people she would be working with, however, I understood her well enough to know that there were several factors already apparent in this new situation that would trigger anger and frustration in her, causing unrelenting stress and sleepless nights, just as her previous position had. This was not due to some personality fault that she should seek to overcome, but arose from her strengths, in particular the way she was stirred by injustice and its effect on people around her.

I suggested she make a list of the scenarios that had most disturbed her in her recent workplace and assess whether she could see them arising in the proposed new position. A day later she phoned to say she was persuaded she should not accept the job because she could see that, although the work itself would bring her joy, the environment would not. She had listened to her life and that gave her a way forward.

---

7. For a short overview see Benner, *Gift of Being Yourself,* 63–68.

ALL ARE CALLED; ALL HAVE A VOCATION; ALL HAVE A VOICE

I am aware that the reminisces I am sharing from the second half of my life when I served as a pastor and later engaged in training and mentoring pastors, have the danger, true of many books written by church leaders, of implying that being a pastor or senior church leader is the pinnacle of Christian service. That is not true. I want to say it again clearly: everyone has a call, not just leaders and certainly not only pastors. God invites and equips women and men to be stewards of this world in a much wider way. God's call to you most probably will be worked out in secular society, carrying out the Creator's mandate to care for people and the earth in the way you are gifted. Your sweet spot may be at work, school, home, sport, church, or your neighbourhood—all places where your deep gladness and the community's deep hunger intersect.

Some people distinguish between *call* and *vocation*, thinking of *call* as Jesus' invitation to disciples to follow him. *Vocation* is then seen as a more specialised invitation to a specific role or form of service which is uniquely yours. The reality is that both words mean the same thing, but *vocation* is a useful term because it reminds us that God has a purpose in giving each of us our specific creation gifts. Those gifts are intended to give us joy (as well as hard work) because our creativity is part of being made in the image of the supreme Creator.

In the final chapter of this book, we will consider the faith in God needed to step out with courage to use your voice. How can you be sure it is God's direction you are hearing? Is this really your vocation? What will this cost you? Telling your personal story and listening to your life—the subjects of these first chapters—are beginning steps along the way to finding that voice so that you can use it. The next step is to see God's invitation to be simply yourself, yet open to the Holy Spirit making you *more* than yourself.

Personal Reflection

"It is not what you and I do . . . It is what God is doing, and he is creating something totally new, a free life!" (Gal 6:15 The Message).

This is the Apostle Paul's reminder to look at what God is doing. Processing everyday events, thoughts and feelings helps us discern the movements of the Holy Spirit in our life.

Take time to reflect daily on what is happening around you and what that tells you about who you are.

Are you familiar with one of the personality tests such as the Myers-Briggs Type Indicator or the Enneagram referred to above? If so, review your results. Or undertake one now.

Then set aside time and invite the Holy Spirit to show you more of who you are created to be and God's agenda for your life.

The ideas and impulses that are God-given often have their genesis months before they come to our attention.

If you journal, read back through what you have written in the past month or two and look for the bigger patterns or the hints about what God is preparing you for.

3

Simply Yourself, More Than Yourself

Now, Lord, with your help, I shall become myself.
—Søren Kierkegaard (1813–1855)

JESUS DID NOT MINCE his words. Twice he said it was unwise to boost ourselves beyond what we actually are. In the first instance, described in Luke 14, we see him in a Pharisee's house with guests who were lobbying for the highest seat at the table. He uses the occasion to point out how foolish they will look if a more distinguished guest arrives and is given the seat of honor above them. In Luke 18 the setting is the temple. In contrast to those who pray ostentatiously to garner others' approval, Jesus commends the despised tax collector whose humility brings him closer to God. At the end of each of these narratives, Jesus says, "For those who exalt themselves will be humbled, and those who humble themselves will be exalted." The Message paraphrase renders his words, "If you are content to be simply yourself, you will become more than yourself."[1]

What does it mean to be content to be simply yourself? Jesus implies that is desirable. One young woman I know was distressed by her tendency to go at things with vigor and abandon. It made people describe her as a bull. "A bull in a china shop?" I asked. "Sometimes I feel like that," she replied. It was the week after I had been in Africa teaching and using the animals mentioned in the previous chapter. Although in Kenya we had to find an

---

1. Luke 14:1, 7–11 and 18:9–14 The Message. Also Matt 23:12 The Message.

animal more suitable than an owl to talk about collaborating wisdom, most cultures know the character of the raging bull. I had a great picture of a bull from that recent session, so I sent it to the young woman. She chose to own it—acknowledging that the bull has its good points as well as its disturbing ones. It reminded me of our team's response in east Africa to the disparaging term sometimes used in the street for white foreigners—*mzungu*. We have adopted the word to describe ourselves in light-hearted moments because somehow that takes the sting out of it. Similarly, owning our character, whatever it is, as God-given, takes away the power of implied disapproval, and acknowledges the Creator's wisdom and grace in giving it to us.

THE REST OF BEING CONTENT WITH YOURSELF

Being *simply yourself* offers much more than just defusing others' criticism, however. Being *simply yourself* is a form of rest. It is being secure in who you are. Whenever people see a group photo, I notice they look first for themselves in it. Then they usually express some reservation or even outright displeasure at how they presented in the captured moment. Does God want us to be always dissatisfied with our self, always wanting us to try to present our self in a better light? The insidious side of social media, especially those such as Instagram which rely on image, is that we never measure up to the ideal we want to present to the world. Can we, can you, be simply yourself and appreciate how God has made you? Can you rest in that?

Psychologist David Benner puts it this way. "The self that God persistently loves is not my prettied-up pretend self but my actual self—the real me." What security there is in that. I am loved by God just as I am. Benner goes on, "but master of delusion that I am, I have trouble penetrating my web of self-deceptions and knowing this real me. I continually confuse it with some ideal self that I wish I were."[2]

One coach that I had in my early days as a leader frequently urged me, as we discussed organisational dilemmas I needed to deal with, to "Trust Jennifer!" It felt wrong to do that. Wasn't I, like all humans, prone to selfishness and error? Wasn't it only God "in whom we trust"? But my coach was reminding me to have the courage to accept who God had made me to be—with my natural abilities and spiritual development as well as my weaknesses—and lean on the Holy Spirit's help in acting on that. Trusting myself was an act of faith that God always delights to generously give the wisdom we ask for (Jas 1:5). Nancy Beach has said of her own leadership apprenticeship,

---

2. Benner, *Gift of Being Yourself,* 57.

"I had to learn what it meant to be fully myself, comfortable in my own skin, and willing to express myself authentically as a woman of faith."[3]

UNDER REPAIR TO BECOME MORE THAN YOURSELF

Rest comes from simply accepting who God has made you to be, but it does not ignore that the Holy Spirit has some repair work to do. Jesus' counsel to be content with being simply yourself is so "you will become more than yourself."[4] God's ongoing purpose when you surrender your life is to transform you into the likeness of Christ, into your full potential. This is not uniformity, a squashing of your individuality (including gender) but a wonderful blossoming of it. "We find our unique individuality only to the extent that we are fully formed in the image of Christ," says Mulholland. "In reality, . . . the image of Christ is the fulfilment of the deepest urges of the human heart for wholeness."[5] This is a life-long adventure. You do not know where it will take you or the challenges along the way, but the paradox is that in accepting who you are in Christ, your potential is opened up beyond anything you could imagine. That is what I think Jesus meant by the humble will be exalted: raising you higher than you could ever design for yourself.

When you first place your life in God's hands, you are acknowledging your Creator owns you. Surrendering your agency can sound harsh, but we know God is the one who in love became human, died, and rose again to open this way to new life. Using a biblical metaphor, God is the master potter realizing through the divine craft what was intended for you. With Jesus you can relax, not because you are perfect but because he loves you as you are and *then* goes on to offer healing for shame and a remedy for defects.

REGENERATION—NEW LIFE AT THE CORE OF YOUR SELF

Regeneration is a good word for this remaking of what God always intended you to be. Australians understand regeneration in the environment. When a drought breaks and the first rain hits the dirt, green shoots appear as if by magic. Or after a bushfire has raged through eucalyptus trees leaving them seemingly dead, new leaves soon shoot out from the limbs and we

---

3. Beach, *Gifted to Lead,* 120.
4. Luke 14:11; 18:14; Matt 23:12 The Message.
5. Mulholland and Barton, *Invitation to a Journey,* 41–42.

celebrate the first signs that there is life in the tree after all. In speaking to the Jewish scholar Nicodemus, Jesus described this new life in people who put their trust in him, as like being born again. Other New Testament words are renewal, new creation, transformation, sanctification, metamorphosis. Being born anew is not just a one-off event but the beginning of a process of change into Christlikeness.

Psychologist Arch Hart writes that we often underestimate the necessary depth of this process of regeneration. It is, he says a "profound and permanent work of grace in the heart."[6] We need to keep trusting the renewing work of the Holy Spirit at the core of our being. It begins when we first give our allegiance to God but continues long after the initial thrill of finding freedom in Christ, as God keeps working in us, prompting changes in our motivations, our choices, our habits, and in our automatic responses to the things that happen to us.

The biblical word for the "self" is *heart*. Dallas Willard calls regeneration through the spiritual disciplines, *renovation* of the heart, a heart "which must be given a godly nature and must then proceed to expand its godly governance over the entire personality."[7] Life-long growth in Christlikeness involves transformation of the mind, feelings, body, and soul as well as the will (spirit, heart) and requires commitment to the discipline of learning from the Master.

Dallas Willard was one of my lecturers at Fuller Seminary and I received an invitation to attend his final conference before his untimely death in 2013. This was at a time in my life when I was starting to experience the "little losses" that are part of growing older. These little losses make you feel like one thing after another is being stripped away from you physically and socially, and you can only expect more losses to come! Willard (joined by John Ortberg at that conference) reminded us that God's regenerating, sanctifying work continues in us till we die if we cooperate with his initiatives towards us. Did we want that on-going renovation of the heart? he asked. The four hundred people present in Santa Barbara that weekend wanted it, and the mood lifted even as we were already mourning the coming loss of our teacher. I certainly wanted it. Here was something in my life that would not decline as I aged. It could actually grow! I could expect God's Spirit to keep forming me to be more like Jesus Christ in the years ahead. And I could anticipate a deepening of my relationship with him.

---

6. Hart, *Me, Myself, and I*, 170.
7. Willard, *Renovation of the Heart*, Loc. 385, Kindle.

GOING ON IN GRACE

If you have had the kind of childhood in which love and acceptance were absent; if you were never able to meet your parents' expectations; or your experience of early adult relationships was fraught with self-doubt and rejection, falling into Jesus' arms as you come to understand his love and sacrifice for you can be wonderful, almost overwhelming. What relief, relaxing into his grace! It is like a meal after being lost in the desert for a month; the unbelievable warmth of home after trudging through deep icy snow; or being reunited with loved ones after a Covid-19 pandemic separation. Knowing we are loved and accepted just as we are, is sheer grace.

The point about grace is that you cannot earn it or even deserve it—only put out your hands and receive it. Who you are is not your achievement. Created, rescued, healed—it is all God's work of amazing grace. Sometimes we think of grace only as God's attitude to us at the beginning of our relationship—the father in Jesus' parable, out on the porch waiting with arms wide open to welcome the prodigal home. And his repeated invitation to the older brother to join the party even though he has ignored his father's previous invitation. But grace continues, like waves relentlessly beating on the shore, wave after wave, grace upon grace for the rest of our lives (John 1:16).

The Apostle Paul, defending his ministry and his God-given authority to those in the church in Corinth who were disparaging him, acknowledged his shameful history of persecuting Christians, as well as his extensive qualifications for leadership. Then he says simply, "By the grace of God I am what I am" (1 Cor 15:10). It was on the Damascus road while he was in the act of vigorously pursuing believers, that Paul first appreciated the grace of God's acceptance and his life was turned around. Now many years later, he credits his perseverance in the face of stiff opposition to that same grace, acknowledging it has brought him to this position of security, and he continues with the words, "and his grace to me was not without effect. No, I worked harder than all of them—yet not I, but the grace of God that was with me."

There is a sense that in regeneration, God through the Holy Spirit is not bringing something new into our life but bringing out what was always there—that divine nature given to the man and the woman at the beginning and to us at our creation. It is recovery and development of *all* we were meant to be.

AWARE WE ARE NOT HOLY OR PERFECT

There is a parable about a wretched man tied up for a long time in the back of a cave, until Jesus comes to liberate him. With his limbs finally released from chains and his saviour leading him to the open mouth of the cave, the man has an overwhelming sense of freedom and relief. He has been rescued! But as he comes closer to the light shining in from outside, he looks down and sees how dirty he is and his emotions plummet. He is still so unclean. His renewed awareness of his predicament takes the edge off his joy at being saved.

You too may experience a renewed sense of unworthiness as you move on from the first delights of God's loving rescue. You realise you are in a relationship with a holy God, and you feel unclean. This is a reminder that grace is needed for the journey with God as well as for its beginning. The rest of being *simply yourself* is not just for the beginning; it is for your continuing life because the Holy Spirit is making you *more than yourself*.

We all know people who never relax when a visitor, even a friend, comes into their house. They are too conscious of what is not clean or tidy to the standard they would like or they notice what they had intended to fix up before it was on view. Their discomfort gets in the way of a relaxed conversation and heart-to-heart sharing. Keeping up a pretense that we are perfect is like that. It is wearing; it saps our vitality. In God's presence, pretending is a waste of energy anyway, because God's discerning eye can penetrate any defense we put up to maintain the fiction about our own godliness.

In one African country I visit people sometimes comment on how I speak warmly of my three daughters-in-law. In their culture, a mother-in-law is never satisfied with the woman who marries her beloved son, and it spoils what bond they might have had. It is not that way with Jesus. You can unselfconsciously enjoy the relationship, even as you know he sees and will have some things to say about your less-than-godly attitudes and actions.

In this journey of finding your voice, we will need to discuss selfishness and pride and in a later chapter. But in considering how simply being yourself gives rest, it is interesting to read Hebrews 4. The writer firstly reminds us of the rest that God enjoyed after the initial creation. Then he describes God's word of truth as a scalpel, penetrating to our inmost being and bringing our subconscious motives to light (Heb 4:12–13). The analogy is how early diagnosis enables a surgeon's scalpel to cut out a tumor, removing the dangerous growth before it leads to death. Being aware of sin is no reason to hate yourself, but it gives you every incentive to consent to surgery, because Jesus' renewing work heals and restores.

TRICKLES OF AFFECTION

In the early days of the Covid-19 pandemic in our area, social isolation restrictions prevented anyone outside a household entering through the front door for many months. This was later relaxed a little and on Mothers' Day that year the rule applying was that one family at a time was allowed to visit. My sister-in-law celebrated her birthday, a major wedding anniversary, and Mother's Day all on that May weekend, but for each visit she could only have one part of her large family stop by to see her. One by one they came. So rather than a great all-in celebration, she describes the weekend as wonderful "trickles of affection." What a lovely expression! God's grace comes to us like that, trickles of affection, with occasional welcome showers!

My childhood experience of my parents' love was very steady, reliable, trickles of affection. Although before I had reached adulthood, we had lived in eight houses in three different states, mostly far from any relatives, and I had attended a total of seven schools, Mum and Dad were anchors. I was comfortable and secure with them, even in rented houses and allocated apartments. Looking back, I can see I took their stability for granted and I was shielded from the disappointments my parents experienced which caused some of these interstate moves. I know now how difficult it must have been for them and so I have been reflecting recently on the two years my father chose to drive me to school every morning.

In the 1960s it was not common for parents to drive their children to school. There were no long lines of cars outside at opening and closing times as there are now. I could have used public transport to get to my out-of-district high school and although I wondered why my father did it, I did not value it as I should have. Today I understand more. I was the oldest child, the only daughter, the one most impacted by our family's frequent moves. My father was a quiet introvert, his love not overtly displayed. But for two years till we moved back to Sydney, we had wonderful daily conversations in the car on all sorts of topics—science, society, Bible, psychology. Within his circle, my father was one of the very early Australian thinkers integrating theology and spirituality and psychology with everyday life. And maybe he already knew, that like him, I bond first with another person discussing ideas, before I let the connection sink to my heart. So what I received on those rides were his daily trickles of affection. Daily, just like God's.

GIVING THANKS

We respond to love and grace best by simply accepting it, luxuriating in it, and giving thanks. I hope my parents knew before they died how grateful I was for the steady start they gave me in life, even as I had to separate myself from them and make my own life. I certainly cannot take credit for choosing my parents well! I know from later pastoral experience how many people do not have such a good emotional and spiritual start to their adulthood.

In a similar way, simply being grateful for your *self*, just as it is, acknowledges that you did not create it, you received your *self* as a gift. Even the understanding that enables you to say *I am simply myself*, is from God. As Benner says, "Self-knowledge is God's gift and not the result of your introspection."[8] Gratitude should be our most fundamental attitude to all of life—for a beautiful sunset, the refreshing sting of sand and surf, the grandeur of mountains, the community of city living, the fresh air of country life. We express this as we say thanks for food on our table and the hands of those who prepared it. We say thanks in worship and will have all of eternity to say it again and again.

In the days when I was making regular visits to an obstetrician, I often marveled at his mantelpiece. It was loaded with gifts from grateful new parents—fathers and mothers whose instincts of gratitude for a new life were curiously directed to the medical intermediary. The birth notice columns of the daily papers and Facebook announcements are similarly full of effusive praise for helpers present at the joyful birth of a child. They tell us that the impetus to say thanks is basic to being human. But what if you have no one to thank? Knowing ourselves loved by the Creator is a great blessing.

Even better, an attitude of *thankfulness* can prompt an attitude of *enough*. Gratitude is the answer when nothing satisfies, and we feel unsettled. Gratitude modifies our insistent cry for more; it reminds us to luxuriate in what we have already received, before looking to see what God will give next. But most importantly, gratitude stops us straining for autonomy from the Creator. The quest for self-sufficiency can make us try, like the first woman and man in the Garden of Eden, to cast off the essential connection to God. By saying thanks, we acknowledge we cannot make it on our own. We are accepting the reconciling work of Jesus and choosing to rely fully on God, the source of all that is good. If you find being grateful sometimes hard, begin with gratitude for the created world, for the birth of children, for friends and family, for worthwhile work, and a chance to play and be at ease.

---

8. Benner, *Gift of Being Yourself*, 68.

But make sure you go on to say thanks for connection to the Giver of your true *self* and treasure the rest and security of being *simply you*.

GRACE GIFTS SO YOU ARE MORE THAN YOURSELF

There is, however, a way in which God intends that you become *more than yourself*. It is through the *spiritual* gifts bestowed by the Holy Spirit. In the previous chapter we focused on the *creation* gifts and found that in listening to our life we come to see more clearly who God has made us to be. It was a deliberate choice not to discuss spiritual gifts in that chapter. Putting space between identifying our creation gifts and going on to consider spiritual gifts is important. We too quickly look for God to supernaturally grant us a spectacular personality makeover or endow us with exciting new spiritual gifts, rather than first go down the path of understanding our self and how we function best. Through the work of the Holy Spirit, you can certainly find new power to love and serve well through spiritual gifts, but you will do that through your total being, and most probably in a manner closely related to your creation gifts.

I remember a scene in the Adelaide Town Hall at a time when John Stott was speaking in various cities around Australia. Someone asked him from the floor if there was a connection between *natural* and *spiritual* gifts. "Of course," he said, "because isn't it the same God who gives both?" That response reminds us of the fundamental connection between creation and spiritual gifts—both kinds of gifts are the work of God. And none are for our own aggrandizement, but for the sake of others.

What is a spiritual gift? It is an expression of God's grace that enables us to both worship and serve, and through the Holy Spirit's enabling, make a difference in people's lives. As we have seen, natural abilities and talents are gifts given by God the Creator, but spiritual gifts are distinguished from these by God's specific purpose and power in their use. They may be for a single occasion, or for just a season or for our entire life of service. A simple example—some people have a natural musical talent. If that musical ability is used by God to bring change to others in a powerful way through the Holy Spirit, it is not just a creation gift but a spiritual gift as well.

God gives these gifts freely and graciously. How we use them varies with our personality and situation and opportunities. But regardless of the specific gift or the manner and extent of God's blessing, each believer can experience the Holy Spirit's power in their life, and through their gift (or many gifts), make a unique contribution to the common good.

I have found that most people welcome a fuller understanding of themselves and their spiritual gifts and how they fit together in the church. Just today, a woman who is worn out from much volunteering, asked if I could help her grasp more clearly where she should be serving God in this season of her life. In his letters, the Apostle Paul uses the human body as a picture of the church to emphasise that we not only relate to God as individuals, but we are also part of the community of believers. Inspired and energized by the Holy Spirit, each of us has a part to play in this Body of Christ, the church, for the glory of God and the good of others. And each time the Apostle Paul teaches this truth, he first mentions the oneness of God the Father, Son, and Holy Spirit.[9] He wants his readers to remember that this work of the Holy Spirit in giving spiritual gifts is to be the basis of unity in the church and he challenges his readers to test the source of their inner drives and attitudes. If the gift is from the Holy Spirit, it will glorify God and promote unity. If on the other hand, asserting a spiritual gift creates division, it is not from God or not being used in the way God intends.

This biblical teaching reminds us that no one need feel inferior, and no one should compete with another over the distribution of gifts. Feelings of inferiority or competition come from failing to appreciate we each have a place in God's plan. You can fully exercise your own creativity, your gifts, your voice, without having to encroach on someone else's territory or be threatened by their creativity. Paul illustrates this by noting that the human body needs a foot as well as a hand, an ear as well as an eye. A hand does not do a foot's job well; an ear cannot see at all! What God enables you to do, cannot be done by someone else. Likewise, you cannot do the job of others who have received different gifts from you!

There is an interesting discussion in 1 Corinthians 12 about the weaker parts of the body getting special treatment. Consider how the skull protects the vulnerable brain, the eyebrows shield the eyes, for example. Paul says the church should be like that—the stronger parts protecting the weaker parts, and the vulnerable organs given special consideration because they are essential to the body. What are the weaker parts of the church body? Could it be those needing support, the sick, or those who do not fit the usual profile of church member? The church is to be a haven for all, welcoming everyone's participation as valued parts of the body. This is encouraging if you feel you have nothing to contribute or you are just keeping your head above water in this season of your life.

---

9. 1 Cor 12, Rom 12, Eph 4.

GIVING THE SPIRITUAL GIFTS NAMES

It is helpful if we can find a way to describe the gift we have been given. In the three key Bible passages, at least twenty spiritual gifts are given names. The lists vary between Paul's letters and overlap. Probably he intended to illustrate rather than name every possibility because the gifts are like the colors of the rainbow—you cannot tell where one color ends and the next begins. Yet though they blend into one another, the gifts are usually recognizable, and each person may have several that connect to each other in a cluster.

Some gifts, especially those associated with leadership, are more obvious because they are used publicly. But there are at least ten more gifts mentioned in Paul's lists that are not just for leaders. Most of these—faith, wisdom, discernment, knowledge, for example—are the result of the bountiful grace all of us receive from God. We should expect to be growing in them through the Holy Spirit. In fact, we should actively seek them. Another set—mercy, service, for example—describe the way Christians are to act towards others. These ten qualities should be common to all godly people, so why are they called *spiritual gifts*? It is because some individuals have an extra God-given ability and effectiveness in one or more of these aspects of Christian life and service. For example, some people have stronger faith than the rest of us and can lead us in great ventures; some have well-developed wisdom, even though we are all urged to ask God for wisdom. We must always remember, however, that the main emphasis for all these gifts is service, not self-expression. Nevertheless, it is wonderful to experience God using us through our spiritual gifts with Holy Spirit power. I hope that is increasingly your experience.

Just as there are tests to help us discern our creation gifts and personality, there are studies and questionnaires you can use to identify your spiritual gifts and so be alert to how God wants you to use them. You can start with the list of the twenty or so gifts in Paul's writing and assess which ones you have seen God bless in your life of service. However, it is even more helpful to ask others who know you well—a friend, supervisor, or small group—to give you feedback on what they have observed of the Holy Spirit's activity in your life. Embryonic gifts will need developing; discipline will be needed for you to work faithfully; but the promise is that "we are God's handiwork, created in Christ Jesus to do good works, which God prepared in advance for us to do" (Eph 2:10). How satisfying that is!

Personal Reflection

Jesus says, "Here's what I want you to do: Find a quiet, secluded place so you won't be tempted to role-play before God. Just be there as simply and honestly as you can manage. The focus will shift from you to God, and you will begin to sense his grace" (Matt 6:6 The Message).

In your imagination, Jesus comes into your quiet secluded place. He is coming towards you with open arms. *Do you see him smile at you? How are you responding to him?*

Can you say thanks for who you are? Can you rest in being who God has made you to be?

Ponder feedback you have received pointing to the spiritual gifts the Holy Spirit has given you for this period of your life.

Do you need to respond to these insights or act to develop your gifts? What steps will you take?

4

Leaving Home

Will you come and follow me
if I but call your name?
Will you go where you don't know
and never be the same?

—John L. Bell and Graham Maule (*The Summons*, Iona Community)

I HAVE HAD A very full life, travelled the world, made a wide range of friends, experienced many things, pushed through some new frontiers, and mostly enjoyed the ride. Through the impetus of my husband's agricultural research, our love of travel and more recently, teaching overseas, I have visited perhaps sixty countries for short or longer periods and lived in seven of them. Often my best learning has been done in the face of new or confronting situations as I have reflected on God and the world along the way. When I have ventured out from the safety of home I have been greatly enriched by the journey.

We often use this word "journey" to describe the pathway our life is taking. It is a useful reminder that we have not arrived while we are still alive and kicking. Others prefer the term "pilgrimage" because it suggests deliberately setting out for a known destination and expecting to be changed in some way by the experience. Both these words remind us that when we come to Christ, we are not instantly made whole or freed of the effects of our emotional heritage or our own past actions. Mulholland suggests that it is our instant-gratification culture that makes us expect to be "zapped" out of our brokenness into wholeness. We are hoping God will dispense qualities of personality and character like a vending machine, and we may express great frustration, even anger, when this does not happen instantly. He adds, "Often our spiritual quest becomes a search for the right technique, the proper method, the perfect program that can immediately deliver the desired results of spiritual maturity and wholeness. Or we try to create the atmosphere for the 'right' spiritual moment, that 'perfect' setting in which God can touch us into instantaneous wholeness."[1]

The wonderful promise is that God *will* heal and re-shape us, but usually the Holy Spirit does this only by a gradual process of transforming us be more like Jesus. It takes time and requires our cooperation. Jesus described becoming his follower as being like a baby, born a second time (John 3), so our spiritual growth is a process of growing from child to adulthood. Some growth is normal "built in" development, some comes from the choices we make of ways to live.

This surrendering the comfort of the known, and of static and familiar habits, this journeying spiritually, I am calling *leaving home*. Whether we think of our life as journey or pilgrimage, both require us to leave home to experience it. It is a necessary step of growth towards all we are meant to be. Leaving home also challenges us again not to think our identity is found solely within our self. In Martin Robinson's words, "How strange it is that so many are drawn to leave home to find themselves. Yet the familiar sometimes obscures the eternal, not because it is not present but because it simply cannot be recognized without the experience of a broader canvas. Those who travel have understood the essential paradox that we cannot truly find the 'I' within until we have found the 'Thou' without."[2]

So you cannot own your uniqueness or find your voice till you leave home—physically maybe, but certainly emotionally and psychologically and spiritually. You must be on a journey.

ROLE EXPECTATIONS LEFT BEHIND

In our family of origin, we have roles we are expected to play. Some arise naturally from our birth order and family composition. I am the oldest child. Many of us with this heritage take on organizing the world around us! We become good managers, even good leaders, but with a strong need

---

1. Mulholland and Barton, *Invitation to a Journey*, 23–24.
2. Robinson, *Sacred Places, Pilgrim Paths*, 11.

to control. Or else we take on the role of caretakers and slip into being co-dependent with those we seek to help. For some of us, our inherited roles are influenced even more dramatically by our parents' background and their life experiences. This was what I discovered as I came to understand my mother and her expectations of me. I saw how it influenced me.

My mother's father was a businessman whose life in the Sydney suburb of Bankstown included a term as mayor. I discovered recently that he even had a street named after him there. He owned shoe stores, and my mother, older brother and younger sisters all worked in them. They credited this family support to saving them during the Great Depression of the 1930s. My mother was a competent businesswoman and when her father opened a new store in a country town, she sometimes went as its first manager. However, what she really wanted was to be was a teacher and all her life regretted that she had had to leave school at fourteen to care for her seriously ill mother. In later teenage years there might have been an opportunity to restart her education, but her father forbad it. He did not approve of women working outside the home! His businesses where she worked were, I suppose, "home"!

In the 1930s my mother accepted the role she was expected to play in her family, not protesting her father's edict. After marriage, she also willingly stayed at home to care for her family, understanding that was expected of a pastor's wife, even though she had little experience or interest in home crafts. Several times she tried to complete high school through night classes to give her the opportunity for higher study but gave up in the interest of my father's very demanding and multiple roles.

Instead, my mother's hopes were invested in me, her only daughter. She ensured I received a good education, starting me in kindergarten at three years old and changing my school mid-primary to give me a better chance of getting a scholarship to the elite public high school in the city where we lived. However, I wonder now whether she realised that the higher education she sought for me would mean I would make different choices from her. I worked outside the home after I had children and she struggled with that.

MORE THAN FAMILY BACKGROUND—CULTURE AND GENERATION

There were cultural overlays to these patterns and choices my mother made, not just expectations from her family of origin. In her generation, independence or self-expression were not given the importance they now have in western society. Individualism today is so valued that a person's desires are expected to take precedence over their role responsibilities. The choices Prince Harry and the Duchess of Sussex have made about where to live and how to function, clearly illustrate a break from the royal tradition of public service that Prince Harry inherited from his grandmother, Queen Elizabeth. This may come from his tragic early life experience, his distance from the throne and being the younger son, but it also reflects generational difference. Members of the generation who were born before 1946 like Prince Harry's grandmother, were raised with a strong sense of duty. Not all seniors uphold these values, but if you are in that oldest generation, sometimes called the "Silent" or "Builder" generation, you are likely to consider discipline and duty more important than self-expression. You let your role in life dictate your expectations.

These generational patterns are important in understanding yourself and those around you. Leaving home will make different demands on you depending on your attitude to your role and responsibilities. If you identify as a Boomer (born 1946 to 1964), you will have lived your life anticipating that your hard work will be rewarded, so you have probably been willing to defer benefits to achieve it. As you approach retirement, however, your personal agenda and your right to a leisured life are also very important to you and you will guard any encroachment on them.

If you are younger than this, a Generation X (born 1965 to 1980)[3] or a Millennial (1981 to 2000), your expectations are vastly different. You feel that it is up to you to choose who you want to be because the world is your oyster, and you have rights.

These are generalizations, of course, and we know it is not as simple as that. You may not fit the stereotype, and perhaps you are one of those who take delight in not being typical. Moreover, the social status of your family and ethnicity also have great influence, affecting your access to education and opportunity, even in Australia where we like to think we have a level playing field.

UNCOVERING YOUR IDENTITY

One of the biggest differences between generations, and influencing your finding your voice, is where you expect your identity to come from. If you are a Millennial or a Gen X you may have grown to adulthood expecting to

---

3. Commentators use various years to define generations. The dividing lines are not significant for this discussion. More important is how your generation influences what you think about the world and life.

find your identity uniquely within yourself, not from any external source such as an assigned role. This is the power behind Elsa's song in *Frozen*, the Disney movie. As she belts out "Let it go" and throws off her royal cloak, she is shedding her role-based identity as oldest princess expected to rule the kingdom after her parents' death. She feels she must reject her inherited identity to find herself in/for herself. The movie has been hailed as an anthem for women's personal autonomy, but interestingly it concludes with Elsa finding she cannot completely dismiss her responsibility to use her personal and inherited gifts for the sake of others.

Tim Keller uses this *Frozen* scenario and Elsa's song to illustrate how today's younger generations truly do expect to find their identity within themselves.[4] But he goes on to argue that individuals who rely on finding their contemporary identity only within their self, will discover it is inherently unstable and fragile, threatened by failure or changed circumstances. Witness how ready famous people are to respond when asked what they would say to their 16-year-old self. They clearly expect they have something to say to that younger self because they have grown or changed since their earlier experience of the world. They are acknowledging that their identity is not located solely within their genes or psyche, but malleable by outside influences and growing wisdom and by life experience.

When a person's identity is thought to be found in what they do, as in work or sport, rather than in a fixed role, it can spill over into workaholism, driving the person to reach for ever higher and higher success to feel good about themself. That can have destructive consequences later. Sportswomen and men seem to experience particular difficulty in adjusting to everyday life when their high-profile identity is lost or at least diminished at the end of a stellar career.

It may be that the apparent increase in anxiety among young people today arises from, or at least is fed by, the pressure to find all they need for life within themselves. For some, this results in rejection of life itself, with tragic consequences.

RIGID ROLE BOUNDARIES ARE ALSO NOT THE ANSWER

Nevertheless, the answer is not to return to the fixed role definitions of old to define our identity. We cannot, nor would we want to, go back to the rigidity of previous generations. We see the straitjacket it imposes on people, particularly on women in most societies.

---

4. Keller, "Identity."

So the process of *finding your voice* involves accepting your identity is not totally fixed, not set in stone or written in the stars, nor the responsibility of the "universe." Your identity *starts* with who God created you to be, your physical traits, your family setting, your opportunities and life events, but develops through cooperation with God's Spirit. The Scriptures teach that our greatest resource is the grace of God, redeeming and rebuilding us as we pursue life in relationship with our Creator/Redeemer. This means that we must make choices, grow in self-understanding and learn to listen to God's promptings from within and without, as we uncover our identity.

Leaving home is a fitting way to describe this process of owning your choice to respond to God's promptings. In many ways, it is a life-long and repeated task, not just one of a teenager-becoming-an-adult. My experience in entering retirement, once again challenged my understanding of who I was, but in a new way, just as becoming a mother or a mother-in-law or a grandmother had done in previous decades. Leaving home implies a willingness to trust what God is doing in your life whatever season you are in. Trusting is the key word here, because you do not know where it will take you in the future.

LEAVING HOME EMOTIONALLY

In some societies leaving home physically does not mean establishing a separate household but it can be a tragedy of exploitation and unfulfilled potential if adult children never take the step of leaving home emotionally. It indicates that they have not reached mature adulthood. The foundation of a good marriage outlined in God's creation plan (Genesis 2), starts with the man leaving home. It applies to the woman too. Ideally, the leaving, the letting go, can be done with love and gratitude to the family who have raised us. We want and need to have a continuing relationship with our parents, brothers, sisters, and other family members, even as other relationships evolve. From the parents' perspective, the teenage years preceding this leaving home can be a process of helping our children transfer their dependence to God, so that the newly adult child finds their developing identity in God.

Even for those who do not acknowledge the Creator, their identity starts with God's creative act and is designed to move through growing awareness of individual uniqueness in teenage years and young adulthood, to establishing the person's confidence in relating to the wider world. Along with that should come a healthy differentiation from family and peers as the person makes a life for themselves. For many people, this may be as far as they can go in the search for their identity. Our Christian hope, however, is that when we search for true life and realise all is not well with our inner being, we discover the good news that we do not have to generate this all-rightness in our self. We do not need to be "enough" or totally self-sufficient. *Enough* comes freely from Jesus Christ, as we inherit his righteousness by a grant of grace. We begin the journey with God simply by putting out our hands to accept grace. That is enough. In New Testament terms, we discover our identity is "hidden with Christ in God" (Col 3:3).

THE GIFT OF OUR SELF-IN-CHRIST

Benner names this redeemed identity a *gift*—we receive the gift of our self-in-Christ. "True identity," he says, "is always a gift from God."[5] And later, "The self we find hidden in Christ is our true self, because Christ is the source of our being and friend of our true identity."[6] He points to 1 Corinthians 15:22b which in The Message is expressed very simply: "Everybody comes alive in Christ."

The Apostle Paul later describes the objective of the spiritual journey as being formed into the image of Christ (2 Cor 3:17–18; Gal 4:19). This Jesus-likeness is both character and identity. It is not a U-turn, turning our back on all we were created to be, but rather moving towards being fully what the Creator designed us for—mature, godly adults.

Giving up the urge to create our own selves and simply receiving our identity as a gift from God, does not create a herd of lookalike zombies or a regime of handmaidens conditioned for a single purpose. We do not lose what God has already created us to be—unique women and men each with our own reflection of the Creator. Coming alive in Christ starts with all we have inherited from our childhood and youth but emerges into its full potential, the flower from the bud, if we cooperate with and give our consent to it.

Unfortunately, some of us do not grasp this opportunity to unfold like a flower in early adulthood. Understanding our unique potential in Christ comes only later in life. For many women, when the pressure of bearing and raising children starts to lessen, the identity question raises its head again and can no longer be pushed away. Perhaps if this is you, it comes from dissatisfaction with where you find yourself after giving the best years of your life to caring for others. If you have never fitted into the pattern expected of adult women, perhaps you are single or childless into your 40s, the realisation that the dream needs to change may come at this mid-life point too.

5. Benner, *Gift of Being Yourself,* 18.
6. Benner, *Gift of Being Yourself,* 84.

Whatever prompts it, leaving home to center your identity in Jesus Christ is a fitting metaphor for the beginning of a new season of life. But it takes courage to hand your life over to God, to go out into the unknown.

THE CHALLENGE ESPECIALLY FOR WOMEN

As a pastor I have witnessed that for some women it is particularly problematic to relinquish their life to God. If their story includes severe neglect in childhood or a partner controlling them through domestic abuse, emotional recovery will be long and difficult. Finally, they grasp their precious reclaimed personhood in their trembling hands, but then shockingly discover that Jesus asks them to hand it over to him! Not easy. It may feel like they are going backwards into darkness again. Nevertheless, in following Jesus we choose to call him Master, not claiming ownership rights over even our own life. Surrendering to him will only be possible if we respect and trust him, knowing as Creator he wants us to unfold into all we meant us to be.

There are other women who find this leaving home very difficult too. If they have had a great relationship with their father, but then moved straight from that security to the umbrella of a husband protecting them from the world, their identity challenge may come much later and in a different form. It happens more rarely now with younger women, but women at midlife can really struggle to be their own person, especially after the children have left home and the hands-on mother role has gone. Their identity feels emptied.

Women who are even older, widowed or divorced in later years and perhaps not having had to manage the external matters of married life at all until then, can flounder and retreat from life on the death of their husband. Or they may shift their dependence onto their adult children. Leaving home is the last thing they want to do. Not all respond this way, of course. There are wonderful examples of women finding unexpected energy and enthusiasm after divorce or widowhood because they discover a new way to live. They chose to embrace their expanded opportunities with zest.

In appreciating the challenge of leaving home to follow the Master, the examples of Jesus' first-century disciples come alive. They left their families, employment, all other expectations, to follow him. It was not only men. Women were in the group that made up Jesus' disciples (Luke 8:1–3). In fact, they were the ones still with him at the foot of the cross and at the tomb (Mark 15:40–41). Some of them had the privilege of being the first witnesses to the risen Christ (Matt 28:1–8) and they were in the upper room in at least one of his post-resurrection appearances (Acts 1:14).

MY LEAVING HOME

I first left home at the age of 22. It was a physical leaving—flying to the United States to marry my fiancé. Landing in America was an exciting adventure, defined by the prospect of the new life and marriage that awaited me. When I look back now, however, I am amazed at how little thought I gave to the consequences for my parents. It was devastating for them to lose their only daughter and not be part of her wedding, and it was six years before they saw me again. The fact that they had done the equivalent themselves twenty years before, moving to Perth from their Sydney home with their young family, would not have made it any easier. It was six years too before they could afford to return to visit family in Sydney. (In the 1950s, Perth, the capital of Western Australia, seemed like the end of the world—six different trains and five days to cross the continent west to east.) On the other hand, maybe their willingness to go west when I was a child prepared me to do the equivalent—cross the world—when I was an adult.

I have since appreciated how many women make a similar crossing to another country, but under much more pressing circumstances, fleeing poverty or violence in their home or nation. More courage is required of them than this leaving asked of me. In my final year of university, my research entailed interviewing fifty Greek families who had emigrated in the previous decade. I met a fascinating sample of Greek wives whose fiancé or husband had preceded them to Australia. At intervals, when enough men had established themselves, the government provided a "bride ship" to bring their partners to join them in Australia. These women quickly and usually successfully took on the expected role of wife and mother, but by the time I interviewed them ten years later, many had still not learnt English or become confident in Australian society. They related to the world outside the home through their husband.

This was true of many other women of my generation, even among those who spoke English and could connect independently with the community. Certainly, for me, the going to America was not a full leaving home because I was coming under the protection of my strong and much-admired husband. All was safe and secure because I had found a man to depend on. Leaving home *emotionally* came twenty years later. Society often misinterprets a woman's mid-life change of direction as optional or self-indulgent. For me it came in the form of an increasingly persistent call to serve in pastoral ministry—not an easy road when at that point all pastors in my denomination were male, and it was assumed that was how God wanted it!

In those years when it was difficult for me be accepted as a pastor because I was a woman, even sympathetic male church leaders regarded God's leadership call to women as an optional extra. They would tell me they were fully committed to seeing God's gifts expressed through women, but in their church they had more important matters to tackle, or they did not want unnecessary controversy. As a result, their fears robbed their church and the community of the Holy Spirit-empowered contribution of those who "hold up half the sky"[7]—the women ready and willing to assume leadership.

I knew from my own experience, however, that for the women thus excluded, this rejection was momentous, because their very hard-won identity was being denied. Most had been on a long journey to understand how the Creator had formed and gifted them. They had wrestled with being different and forced against their personality to challenge cultural and church expectations. But even in churches that endorsed women as pastoral carers or chaplains or missionaries, the role of pastor was often seen as a step too far and most doors were shut.

ANOTHER LEAVING HOME

When I look back on my decision to pursue pastoral ministry, I am amazed at how much this was a leaving home too. I did it in concert with my husband because there is no God-honoring other way to do it. Together we sought the safety and wisdom of a counsellor to face its implications. My husband was afraid that I was "going out on a limb" (his words) in challenging the status quo and he feared he would not be able to protect me from the hurts and rejections that would come along the way. But together we chose to trust God's guidance and to follow his leading.

In this connection I have been pondering the parallels to the Old Testament story of Rebekah (Gen 24). She was invited to leave home for a new life in Canaan to marry a man she had never met. Isaac, Abraham's very precious son and heir, needed a wife. The aging patriarch wanted to make sure his son's wife and the mother-to-be of his descendants was in the line of promise, chosen from among relatives back in the country he had come from. So he sent his trusted assistant to find a wife. The servant identified a test to be sure he had God's guidance on this weighty assignment, and it successfully identified a woman of forethought and kindness. Negotiations began with her family to release her to travel back with the servant to marry into Abraham's family. This is not an uncommon story for women

---

7. This cryptic expression was used by Mao Zedong to acknowledge the contribution of women to the new China, and later adopted for the title of a significant book by Kristof and WuDunn on the importance of educating women in reducing poverty in majority world countries. In 2020 Graham Joseph Hill used it in his book making the biblical case for women leading and teaching in the church.

in patriarchal societies where they have few rights, and most decisions are made for them by parents or other relatives.

Rebekah however is given a choice about this marriage, and she says yes. We have to admire her courage. How much did she know of what she was going to? Was Isaac in whom so much had been invested by his parents going to be easy to live with? Would her opinions, clearly recognised in her family of origin, be respected by the new family? We do not know, and neither could she.

There are parallels to God's invitation to Mary to be the mother of God-in-human-form. We might plaintively ask, "Mary, did you know?" but she understood it would be costly. God's invitation to leave the safety of home is never coercive. It asks our cooperation. At an earlier time, Abraham was described as leaving home in faith, not knowing where he was going (Heb 11:8). This now applies to his daughter-in-law Rebekah. In many ways we can identify with her.

Encouragingly, the inner dynamic of sensing God's invitation to something new can overcome our hesitation. One woman I met recently was struggling to find the faith to respond to the possibilities God was opening for her in midlife now her children were grown. In the course of conversation, she mentioned how in her twenties when she was single, she had made multiple trips into a closed country carrying Bibles. She was more fearful now because she had lived the twenty or so years since those early adventures in the shadow of her husband's ministry. She needed to re-capture that daring to leave home again metaphorically. I believe she will.

There are many different seasons in our life, and we will look at these in more detail in chapter 9. At each one we are called to leave the safety of home and explore more of who we are in Christ. Each stage has its own invitations and its challenges. We may have successfully navigated the previous stage but now a new one is opening up. Entering marriage? So much adjustment needed now. Raised your children? Then welcome to the freedom of the empty nest. Retiring? The many issues about purpose and trajectory will arise again, but as the psalmist says hauntingly, "Bring me back from gray exile, put a fresh wind in my sails!" (Ps 51:12 The Message).

RETIREMENT

When I was in my early sixties and my husband a little older, we decided to do retirement officially and together. We marked the occasion with a three-month wander by four-wheel-drive vehicle around the north of Western Australia—a wonderful experience. But when we got back to Perth, we sold the vehicle. That journey was over. What came next? My husband had many invitations to assist younger colleagues and students in their research. In fact, he was soon acting as a part-time interim director of a research centre at the university. For me, God had been putting on my heart a passion for women pastors in developing countries. I saw this as using the multiple experiences I had of living overseas, and twenty years of pastoring and lecturing in Perth. It also offered me a way to teach short-term in different countries while still having time for my grandchildren at home. There were already five of these precious little girls and boys and more were expected. The next stage of my journey with God had begun. But I had to respond to the call and leave home, discovering again my identity in Christ for this new chapter.

Personal Reflection

Are you familiar with C. S. Lewis' *Chronicles of Narnia* stories? Four children are given the opportunity to leave their country home (via a wardrobe) to enter the land of Narnia, an imagined world of evil witches, mythical figures and talking animals. At first, they understand very little of what it all means, but then they meet Aslan, the fierce lion. He is gentle with them but never a push-over and they come to discover him as the Jesus-figure who is always calling them to "come up higher" because they need to have faith in him to enter into all he has in store for them. Over the seven books of the series, they are entrusted with considerable responsibility, reigning as queens and kings and fighting battles as they combat evil and participate in Aslan's restoration of Narnia to its intended beauty and peace.

Even by the last book, when much of what has gone before is starting to make sense, they still need to trustingly follow Aslan's call to "come up higher." They overcome evil and find total reality only at the end of the story. We too may only understand our lives fully when we meet Jesus face to face.

Explore the theme of leaving the familiar, like the children in Narnia, for an unknown destination in your own life.

Have you heard Jesus' invitation to adventure? More than once? What has he asked of you?

Are you hearing another prompting now? Are you willing to trust this gentle, strong Aslan lion Master and come up higher?

5

Imposter Syndrome

We ask ourselves, Who am I to be brilliant, gorgeous, talented, fabulous? Actually, who are you not to be? You are a child of God. Your playing small does not serve the world. There is nothing enlightened about shrinking so that other people won't feel insecure around you. We are all meant to shine, as children do. We were born to make manifest the glory of God that is within us.

—Marianne Williamson (*A Return to Love*)

MARIANNE WILLIAMSON IS AMONG many in the self-help community who urge us to stop thinking of ourselves as small and inconsequential. It is useful to let the unabashed positivity of her words shock us into re-assessing how we think of ourselves. Regularly devaluing or denying our abilities has been called the *imposter syndrome*. This includes the feeling when we are invited to contribute, that we are a fraud in imagining we can perform the task, and what is worse, sooner rather than later we will be found out. Research back to 1978 when the term was first used, has shown that women, especially high achieving women, are particularly prone to this.[1]

In the business world, Sheryl Sandberg, Chief Operating Officer of Facebook, has observed that in contrast to men who will usually attribute their success to their own effort, women underestimate their contribution, and credit whatever they have achieved to other factors. They are often reticent

---

1. Clance and Imes, "The imposter phenomenon," 241–247.

to promote their own value and negotiate a position or salary raise. In an explosive TED Talk in 2010, she urged women to take their rightful place at the table and lean in to opportunity. *Lean In* subsequently became the title of her 2015 international bestseller in which she explores why women so often feel a fraud when they are simply using their abilities. Australian Crabb's more recent book, *The Wife Drought,* addresses the same phenomenon.

A SEAT AT THE TABLE

Taking a seat at the table is an expression that also received traction from Sandberg's TED Talk. In her book, she describes a scene that many of us can identify. In fact, we have probably participated in it and reacted the same way. A group of people attend a small meeting in a room where the expectation is that everyone sits around the conference table. Some hang back, however, seeing if there are enough seats or food at the table. Most often, these are the women, and their body language suggests, not just consideration of others, but an uncertainty about whether they have a right to be at that table.[2]

Christians are called to practice humility like Jesus (Phil 2:3–5). But often we do not know what humility looks like, thinking it means being reticent to use our gifts or serve in a way that draws attention to our self. Richard Foster describes humility as *power under control.*[3] True power, he says, is creative, loving, and teachable and badly needed in our world. This means it is not humility to ignore the everyday promptings of the Holy Spirit or decline the larger opportunities to serve God. That kind of mistaken humility can even lead us to envy others who are seizing the opportunities God sends their way.

The imposter syndrome also raises its head when, after helping someone through deep conversation or a public talk or counselling, we rerun the activity in our minds and notice all the things we could have done better. Moreover, if someone thanks us, saying how helpful it was or how God had spoken to them through it, rather than just acknowledging that, we are at pains to point out the deficiencies we have identified. We devalue what God is doing through us. I remember Dallas Willard saying that when he had given a public address or sermon, as he left the venue, he let his contribution rise up like a balloon into the sky as an act of thanks to the Creator for the gift given him. I still picture him in my mind walking out to his car, releasing the "balloon." I try to do it too.

2. Sandberg, *Lean In*, 27–30. See also Long, *Seat at the Table.*
3. Foster, *Money, Sex and power*, 202.

Nancy Beach suggests if we are going to improve our leadership, we do need to ask ourselves questions and seek feedback from others to improve our skills, especially in communication.[4] But this is very different from continually underestimating our contribution.

MISSING THE OPPORTUNITIES

Unfortunately, we can also let imposter syndrome block the larger opportunities that might have been ours. In the first church where I served on a pastoral team, I was breaking new ground for women and my title and role did not reflect what I was actually contributing. At several junctures, the elders suggested re-examining my position, but for the first three years of my appointment to that church, we had no senior pastor. So every time the subject of my role was raised, I demurred, saying that finding a senior pastor was a more important priority. To be truthful, I was also afraid of the controversy. After several years, when I resigned to travel with my husband to Europe for his research sabbatical, my position had still not been resolved. My reticence to address this did not serve me or any women successors well.

More recently, false humility nearly lost me another valued recognition. This one I can still laugh at. An email came from the Governor-General of Australia, but I did not open it, thinking it was a scam. Why would he be contacting me? We are rightly suspicious of emails from unknown or unexpected sources. Fortunately, my husband had been asked some background information on his wife a year earlier so without explaining why, he suggested I should not ignore the communication but open it. He was right. The email informed me I was being considered for an Australian honour and if I was agreeable to receiving it, they would continue with the selection process. Nearly missed out on that one!

My mother followed an even more dramatic path. In the 1950s my father was head of a Bible College and granted a year's leave to finish his doctorate in San Francisco. He could not afford to take his family with him and so we stayed behind in Perth. A week or so before he sailed, the man who was to oversee the functioning of the college while my father was absent, died. In the emergency, my mother moved us all into the residential college and acted as dean for the year my father was absent. As I mentioned in the previous chapter, she had been a businesswoman until well into her 30s, with considerable managerial experience, but it had lain dormant for many years. We and the college survived the year very successfully, but when my father returned, my mother went back to her quiet home role. Who she was

---

4. Beach, *Gifted to Lead*, 109–110.

and what she could do was again hidden because of her (and the Christian community's) expectations of a good Christian wife and mother. It was Australian society's expectation too at that time.

A friend, also a pastor's wife, took a different route a generation later and in another city. She began further study to become a clinical psychologist once her children were in school. This was at considerable emotional cost because the expectation of her church was that she be totally available to do the things the pastor's wife was traditionally supposed to do—run the women's group, provide pastoral support to hurting people in the community, entertain in the church manse etc. Some of these she certainly did, but not all of them while she studied and later practiced as a clinical psychologist. She felt the condemnation keenly.

Community disapproval is a major reason women hold back from claiming their seat at the table. We are socialized to fit in, to maintain the peace, to not cause controversy. As I have described previously, when my husband and I had discussions about my changing course to train for pastoral ministry, his concerns were about the emotional cost of the struggle that would ensue. He knew how difficult it would be for me to be exposed to criticism and examination of my motives. And he was correct. When disapproval focusses on us for using our God-given gifts, it is an attack on our identity—the very core of our being. Very painful.

AMBITION

One relative used to say to me when I was young, "Be good, sweet maid, and let who will be clever." I understood it as an instruction to keep my intellect hidden so that people would like me. Yet in every other way, I was encouraged to use what gifts I had been given. Nancy Beach references research showing that though women now have wider access to education and are permitted to shine in their accomplishments, this advancement is only acceptable if their goals are "selfless."[5] Ambition is grudgingly acceptable to drive women forward, but it is apparently unacceptable to want to be appreciated and recognised for their accomplishments. Beach adds, "Women who are ambivalent about their leadership will tend to shrink back, express their points of view with some tentativeness, and second-guess not only their instincts, but their right to make a leadership contribution."[6]

A mentor whom I greatly respected once told me I was too ambitious. I suspected it had to do with my being a woman. We were working together

---

5. Cited in Beach, *Gifted to Lead*, 74–75.
6. Beach, *Gifted to Lead*, 75.

on a project and he was a man with world-wide recognition and achievements—clearly ambitious himself. Upset at his criticism, I scurried home and did a search of the Scriptures to see if God considered ambition a bad thing. What I found made me question my mentor's opinion—equally painful because I had received and appreciated his support up to that point. But the Bible is clear that in every instance where "ambition" is considered damaging to the person or the community, it has the qualifier "selfish" in front of it. All of us need to examine ourselves to root out selfish ambition, men as well as women, but wanting to use our gifts compassionately and well is not selfish. In Buechner's words, when our service brings together the way we are wired and need in the community, it gives us deep joy.

Commenting on the Christian understanding of faith from Hebrews 11, Ted Gibson observed:

> It is quite difficult to distinguish between personal ambition and the purpose of God. God puts you into a place for the purposes of growth. But never fall foul of the silly idea (which is quite unbiblical) that you don't have to do anything, you just wait on God and He will do everything. God's commission is work: "Be fruitful, fill the earth, grow, take over." So growth is written within the very fibre of biblical faith. Spiritual growth within ourselves, growth of souls, growth in the work of God, are His order. Yet the ego can be wrapped up in that anticipated growth. Therein lies our problem.[7]

He went on to add:

> So we need to distinguish human ambition from divine vision. The way to keep yourself from failure here is to make sure that the growth of the soul accompanies the fulfilment of the vision. Growth in me as well as growth in the program of God is vital.

GENDER AND SHALOM

Much of the discussion elsewhere of the *imposter syndrome* is a comparison between men and women, some claiming it arises from competition between men and women. Encouraging women to grasp the opportunities available to them is interpreted as a threat to men, especially to those who currently hold the power.

Lisa Sharon Harper has written a delightful book about how God's "very good" creation is expressed in *shalom*—the big Hebrew word for

7. Turner and Ingram, *Life in the Spirit*, 15.

completeness, well-being, abundance.[8] Starting from Genesis 1, she surveys the wonder of God's intention of wholeness for a good world and its people. This wholeness, this *shalom,* is a relationship word, embracing the oneness of the Creator with people; the relationship between these people as man and woman; and with the world over which they are given stewardship. Unfortunately, Genesis 3 makes it clear that before long, all these relationships were affected by human rebellion against God's sovereignty.

In one significant chapter, Harper addresses *shalom* between genders. She says that when women hide who they are created to be, some of it still peeps through, and men react as if threatened. The *shalom* between genders that was God's intention is sadly missing. Harper writes as an African American woman whose ancestors did not know *shalom* in the plantations of southern slavery. She did not know it herself when subjected to violation in her youth and later excluded from leadership in her church. But she strongly asserts the "very good gospel," the good news of Jesus, is God's way of restoring *shalom.* God can restore all our relations: with the Creator, with the world, but also between men and women. Reconciliation—restoration, recovery—is God's intention. No wonder we hunger for it.

There are two sides to this gender divide. No side can be fully restored if its counterpart is not restored. Men need women to enter fully into God's blessing, just as much as they need it for themselves. And women need men as partners in God's world, not competitors. Attaining this *shalom* must be something we intentionally work at. But how? What part must women play in this?

THREE DIVIDING WALLS

Gender is one of three fundamental human power relationships, and one of three hurtful divides that reconciliation can address. The Apostle Paul lists these three as ethnicity, slavery and gender in his encompassing statement to the Galatian church. "So in Christ Jesus you are all children of God through faith, for all of you who were baptized into Christ have clothed yourselves with Christ. There is neither Jew nor Gentile, neither slave nor free, nor is there is male and female, for you are all one in Christ Jesus" (Gal 3:26–28). The level ground under the cross should leave no place for competition between Christians, no envy of the other, no ignoring the other. But the reality is, when trust is lost, walls of hostility are built and something more is needed. That is God-given *peace,* the New Testament word for *shalom* wholeness and reconciliation.

8. Harper, *The Very Good Gospel.*

Preachers and writers often speak of *peace with God* to describe the salvation that comes through Jesus. We experience it with joy when we come to God in confession and submission and accept his grace offer of new life. But the reconciliation that begins in Jesus also initiates the process of restoring peace between people, and wonderfully, can include *peace* between genders.

THE FIRST DIVIDING WALL COMES DOWN

For the first-century Christian church proclaiming oneness in Christ, the immediate test was the divide between Jews and the outsider Gentiles. Paul reminds the Ephesians, "For [Christ] himself is our peace [shalom], who has made the two groups one and has destroyed the barrier, the dividing wall of hostility . . ." (Eph 2:14). This inclusive dynamic of the gospel, bringing Jew and Gentile together, had to be learned and practiced by the early church in the harsh reality of their everyday lives. The challenge was to embrace those Christians who were not first Jews—to affirm that they were also rightfully accepted into God's kingdom.

The book of Acts documents that this did not happen overnight. First, the apostolic leaders had to be primed so that they would recognise the full implications of gospel reconciliation. For this step, God prepared Peter by a roof-top vision to break tradition and enter the house of Cornelius, a non-Jew, and tell his whole household about Jesus. Afterwards Peter reported back to the Jerusalem apostles that the witnesses saw the Holy Spirit fall on this group of Gentiles, just as on the Jews at Pentecost. This was convincing evidence that inclusion of the Gentiles was God's idea and that *shalom* between ethnic groups was possible.

When a growing number of Gentiles then became Christians in distant Syrian Antioch, the witnesses this time were Barnabas and Paul. The Jerusalem leadership received and trusted their evidence that this movement too was of God. Persuaded by the Holy Spirit activity, they further endorsed the inclusion of Gentiles in the church and communicated their growing understanding that this was a new work of God. I sometimes wonder, if the Jerusalem Council of Acts 15 had been held before the leaders had seen the Holy Spirit's blessing of the Gentiles, the traditional view of Jewish exclusivity might have prevailed, and Gentiles excluded even before the gospel could spread out further from Jerusalem.

Making room for others in the tent is not easy. It involves giving up personal or social or gender self-interest to demonstrate the reconciling power of the gospel. The inclusion of Gentiles, for example, had later to be defended publicly by Paul on several occasions. And he went to great lengths to demonstrate it in practical terms by his campaign to collect aid from the Gentile churches to bring to the famine-hit Jerusalem Christians, even as the centre of Christianity moved away from their city into Gentile territory and the church leadership with it. This was necessary, however, as only then could the gospel and its reconciling power finally be seen to go into the whole world.

THE SECOND WALL—SOCIAL EXCLUSION (SLAVERY)

We see repeated the same pattern of reluctance to embrace the other two groups behind "dividing walls"—slaves and women—as full members and leaders in the Body of Christ. It continued to be a challenge for the church to embrace God's inclusive *shalom* and break down of the walls of hostility surrounding each of those divisions. The Jew-Gentile divide was the first, but its resolution in *shalom* is the model for these other two divides as well.

Unfortunately, overcoming the second "dividing wall of hostility"—slavery—took a long time. The seeds of reconciliation were obvious in the way first-century Christians were instructed to treat servants and slaves as their brothers and sisters in Christ. Slaves were included in church gatherings and later in leadership, but full liberation took many centuries, far too many centuries. The nineteenth century emancipation movement in England was led by Christians, although even then some in the church opposed change in the social status of slaves, fearing the economic consequences and making an appeal to a perceived divine hierarchical order of society. The abolition of slavery in North America was an even greater upheaval. That battle is still far from totally won in many parts of the world today, and we need to be continually encouraged to open our arms to the economically non-free, whether we see them as slaves in closed factories or as refugees from oppression.

THE THIRD WALL—HOSTILITY BETWEEN MEN AND WOMEN

However, our focus here is the third wall of hostility—the competition and lack of trust between genders, because that is surely what lies beneath the imposter syndrome and the reticence of women to take their seat at the table. What will it take to allow Christ to be our peace here too? If we follow the pattern of Christians challenged at the birth of the church to reconcile between Jew and Gentile, the first step is to see what God through the Holy Spirit has *already* been doing.

Against the traditional patriarchy of the time, the New Testament recounts the first-century contributions of women such as Pricilla and Phoebe and Lydia and Junia and the daughters of Philip, as well as the women who travelled as Jesus' disciples in his earthly ministry and were trusted witnesses of his resurrection. Later, women have figured prominently among the writers and teachers of Christian spirituality down through the centuries. Florence Nightingale and Catherine Booth and many educators have led significant practical change benefiting all of society. There is also a long tradition of women serving as missionaries in faraway places, and they have clearly been blessed by God in their faithful and creative endeavours. Many of their spiritual daughters in the majority world have now founded or lead caring organisations and churches.

So what about in the west? Just as the Jerusalem church leaders were compelled to re-examine the Scriptures in the light of the Holy Spirit blessing on the Gentile converts, so today God's evident endorsement of the gifts given to women should cause all sections of the church to look again at the New Testament as it witnesses to the service and leadership of women. It is significant that in the book *How I Changed my Mind about Women in Leadership: Compelling Stories from Prominent Evangelicals*[9] many of the well-known leaders and scholars who contribute a chapter were moved to re-examine their understanding of the gender divide in the light of Scripture when they saw God-given gifts of leadership in their wife, daughters or other women close to home.[10]

The poor witness to gospel reconciliation between genders in the church is a scandal. But opening up space for women to use their gifts applies not only within the church. In all spheres, the more powerful and the privileged should make room for those struggling to respond to God's call and gifting. This includes creating opportunities for women to serve inside and outside the church, offering mentoring, apprenticeships and specific activities, and welcoming them as partners in whatever endeavour they are engaged in. If we truly believe the very good gospel brings peace and overcomes barriers, then we need to be demonstrating it between the genders in society as well as in the church. Christians should be leading this movement of inclusion, not resisting it. But it also requires women to take risks and come out of hiding.

---

9. Johnson, *How I Changed my Mind.*

10. For a succinct discussion of women's gifts and leadership in New Testament times, see Hill, *Holding up Half the Sky.*

WHY DO WE HIDE?

Why do we hide, pretending through this imposter syndrome that we have little to contribute? Three reasons, I think. Firstly, we are afraid of challenging entrenched power because that power can be dangerous if it is used against us physically, emotionally, financially, or psychologically. It is a small illustration, but I was explaining to my husband recently why when I am on my own, I immediately lock the car door when I get into it, especially at night. We now live in a relatively safe city, so he thought my action was unnecessary. But a lifetime of living in more dangerous countries, but especially a lifetime of being a woman, has trained me to be vigilant. Is that unnecessary?

In a recent workshop aimed at helping men understand what it is like to be a woman, the presenter asked participants what they did to avoid being raped whenever they walked down a street. What did they look out for? Some of the men had strategies to profile someone walking towards them, assessing if they were big, angry, belligerent, or drunk, but the assumption of an implied threat from all men to all women came as a shock to most. Many gained a new sense of the vulnerability of women in a world where power is not equally shared. Women can choose to develop sensible and routine precautions to live confidently in this world with God's help, but the temptation for most of us is to not press the boundaries. We play safe, opting out of using our freedoms and abilities.

Secondly, our culture, perhaps all cultures, put a high value on a woman being liked. As Sandberg documents in the business world, women who stand out from the crowd are not seen as likeable. That limits both their effectiveness and their promotion prospects. "Bossy" is one of the most damaging descriptions applied to a woman, while for a man the word used might be "strong" or "determined" for the same act—clearly positive adjectives. Pioneering new paths is never easy, and when a woman is told her service is threatening someone else, or making her unpopular, she is inclined to retreat as if the blame rested on her.

Thirdly, women have, whether innately or through enculturation, a strong impetus to protect others by maintaining peace, often at the expense of their own welfare, thinking it is for the greater good. Usually, it is not. In their influential study (mentioned in an earlier chapter) of the impact of oppression on women and girls in many countries, Pulitzer Prize-winning husband and wife team Nicholas Kristof and Sheryl WuDunn show that the most effective way to lift a community out of poverty is to educate its girls.[11] Enough to eat, a roof over your head and freedom from exploitation should be a minimum in any society but when they are extended to young women through education, everyone benefits as the women make their full contribution. It is the same for us too. The "good" we provide is much more than for ourselves. It benefits everyone.

COME OUT OF HIDING!

So what is the antidote to imposter syndrome? In one sense this whole book is a call for you to do your part, come out of hiding, find your voice, and grow in confidence to use it as the Creator intended when you were endowed with divine likeness and received a mandate to care for the world. We know it is good for us all personally because it is God's creation purpose for his daughters as well as his sons. It also can contribute to healing the gender divide that the first man and women fell into, blaming each other for their sin. In her chapter in *Emboldened* on overcoming the imposter syndrome, Tara Beth Leach suggests that we arm ourselves with Jesus' promise that *all believers* will do even mightier works than he did.[12] This is a great call to faith, the quality that Jesus urges us all to have because it expresses confidence, not in ourselves, but in the God who empowers us. When we use that power, it should be the kind of power Jesus had—infused with compassion.

Richard Foster in discussing power and the discipline of obedience reinforces this motivation. He says we owe it to both God and people to serve them with the gifts God has given us. "How do we serve others in the world? We serve them by preparing ourselves to lead and by accepting the opportunity to lead when it is offered. Our world is hungry for compassionate, servant leaders."[13] That is indeed godly, not selfish, ambition.

Personal Reflection

"Readily recognize what [God] wants from you, and quickly respond to it. Unlike the culture around you, always dragging you down to its level of immaturity, God brings the best out of you, develops well-formed maturity in you" (Rom 12:2 The Message).

Lisa Sharon Harper concludes her chapter on *Shalom Between Genders* quoting an older, wiser women who said to her, "Lisa, you will flourish

---

11. Kristof and WuDunn, *Half the Sky*.
12. Leach, *Emboldened*, 40, quoting John 14:12–14.
13. Foster, *Money, Sex and Power*, 243.

when you stop apologizing for your power and live fully into the woman God created you to be."[14]

Do you have someone who can say that to you? Ask them to remind you (as often as necessary) who God has made you to be and let them walk with you as you step out with courage.

Or maybe you need to respond to an opportunity you already have. Perhaps someone is making space for you, inviting you in. They will applaud you as you take your place at the table. Pull up your chair!

---

14. Harper, *The Very Good Gospel,* 101.

6

Body People, Resurrection People

No matter what you pay, or how carefully you assemble the materials, you are not going to create a human being . . . The only thing special about the elements that make you is that they make you. That is the miracle of life. We pass our existence within this warm wobble of flesh and yet take it almost entirely for granted.

—Bill Bryson (*The Body*)

USING OUR VOICE IS a physical act. In fact, everything we do is through our physical bodies. This means that our attitude to our bodies is important. Not only are we called to love them as God's creation but care for them according to the instruction manual we have been given. For women, this is especially important, because we have sometimes been told that our very Creator-given bodies are the reason we cannot serve God fully or in the public sphere; that we cannot find a voice that will be heard by others.

THE SPIRITUAL IS CONNECTED TO THE PHYSICAL

Two years ago, before Covid-19 stopped international travel, I was teaching in the Mau mountains. The Kenyan high country is where some of the world's best distance athletes train at altitude. Working their lungs hard in the rarefied air increases their efficiency in using oxygen and stimulates the production of more red blood cells—so necessary to get everything they can out of their bodies under the pressure of international competition. The women I was working with were not athletes in that sense, but they were athletes in the use of their lungs because every day they walked great distances at this altitude with their cows, across fields to get to pasture, then back home and to anywhere else they needed to go.

We were using material from an African course on healing from trauma.[1] It emphasises that through Jesus' death and resurrection there is a difficult but very real possibility of recovery from the kind of trauma many of these women have suffered. Sessions can be very demanding, particularly when the women have not previously been encouraged to talk about the impact of violence in their lives. After the second session, I introduced an exercise from the course, teaching how to focus on your breathing for a few minutes to help you take control and relax when overcome by strong feelings.

As I explained through the interpreter what we were going to do, the women began to laugh. Try as I might, I could not find out why at each step they were laughing instead of taking deep slow breaths. Overnight I consulted the leaders. Apparently, they thought I was saying they had poor lungs and needed treatment. Nothing could have been further from the truth! I reassured them that they had superior lungs! So next day with a much longer explanation, including telling them that I lived for a time in a very polluted Asian city, and so in contrast to them I have very poor lungs, I tried again, but with only moderate success. Somehow, they could not see a connection between our discussion of the Holy Spirit's healing work in their lives and their physical bodies.

This was again apparent in a similar setting in Uganda. Some of the team questioned introducing a breath technique for reducing anxiety into a Bible teaching session. Practical ways of managing stress and panic are part of most counselors' work with their clients, and the exercise I was suggesting was a very simple one. But the disquiet of both the women and my colleagues highlighted to me the divide we have made between body and spirit in our thinking.

In the next chapter, we will focus on some aspects of what it means to be a woman—to have a woman's body. But if we are to enjoy being women and address the claims of women being "the weaker sex" with its implications for using our gifts, we must first think about what it is to be physical beings—human beings God made "very good" in the creative act at the beginning. We must consider our connection with our bodies.

---

1. Hill et al., *Healing the Wounds of Trauma*.

WHAT IS IT THAT LIVES ON AFTER DEATH?

Birth might seem an obvious place to start in contemplating human physical existence, but death is also a valuable touchstone, because the act of dying confronts us cruelly, bringing the body into focus. That is why for Christians, Jesus' resurrection is so important, and so is our own.

Surveys show that even in skeptical western societies, most people have an expectation of some kind of life beyond death.[2] A life *after* life. But what people think lives on is quite varied. Is it the same person, or just their soul or spirit that exists beyond the grave? Or maybe only a conscious brain? As we struggle to describe in everyday language a pathway through this minefield, the important thing Christians must avoid is a false body-soul dichotomy, even though that understanding has found its way into some of our Christian burial liturgies.

I have often heard it said, "We now say goodbye to this body which he no longer needs." These words may be important for loved ones struggling to accept the reality before them, words that mark the finality of death as far as earthly existence is concerned, but now I do not use them. A day came when I realized they were misleading, even for Christians who know that the Scriptures teach the expectation of a bodily resurrection. Similarly, the traditional words, "We come together . . . to dispose reverently of the mortal body," if they are not followed by words such as "confident of the resurrection to eternal life,"[3] can suggest we are discarding something which has served merely as the casing for an immortal soul and is not needed any more.

So what is it that lives on after death? Some indeed do think it is only our brain and propose a purely mechanistic view of human consciousness, with no soul in sight. Francis Crick, building on his Nobel Prize-winning double helix reputation, declares in his *The Astonishing Hypothesis: The Scientific Search for the Soul*, "You, your joys and sorrows, your memories and your ambitions, your sense of personal identity and free will, are in fact no more than the behaviour of a vast assembly of nerve cells and their associated molecules."[4]

This "nothing but" school of thought understands the brain as the essence of the person—a brain which finally will be fully understood and whose data could then be downloaded into software for a kind of eternal existence. Or the brain itself could be replaced by a transplant. Reflecting on this, one wag enquired, "When a person has a brain transplant who wakes

---

2. McKnight documents some of these in *The Heaven Promise*.

3. Wording from a Funeral service in Baptist Union of Great Britain, *Patterns and Prayers*.

4. Crick, *The Astonishing Hypothesis*, 3.

up?" In other words, what is the person? Where are the relationships? Who is the human being created in the image of the relationship God?

On the other hand, Scripture does not propose an immortal soul living in a perishing body, with just the soul having an after-life. If we think a *soul* is better off without a body, then it looks like the *soul* is at war with the *body*. This body-soul split unfortunately came to influence Christian thinking in the first and second centuries through the Gnostics. They thought all matter, including the body, was evil, trapping the spirit.

Gnosticism has returned more recently in New Age thinking through the reintroduction of concepts of reincarnation in which the soul inhabits a succession of bodies until absorbed into the One, into depersonalized consciousness. When the body is seen as simply the carrier of the soul, the body does not matter and so you can do what you like with it. Where does that leave moral choice? Or proper and just treatment of other people's bodies?

RESURRECTION OF OUR HUMAN BODY IS A CORE CHRISTIAN BELIEF

Christians understand the Scriptures to declare that after death, the body through which we touch and feel, is resurrected. The Anglican Book of Common Prayer calls this "the sure and certain hope of the resurrection to eternal life." Our bodily resurrection will be a magnificent transformation of the whole person, in the same way in which Jesus' body was transformed. We will live through those transformed bodies for an eternity of deep joy.

The Bible pictures this life after death in God's presence as a wonderfully rich feast. I remember a young man whose wife was tragically killed in a car accident on their honeymoon, speaking at her funeral in our church and saying, "We'll take a rain-check on that dinner date. Save us some seats at the banquet." The scene still brings tears to my eyes with its mingling of pain and hope.

When my own mother died, my family were present at her bedside and experienced that same blending of grief and joy. She had been only a shadow of her former self for many months as she wasted away in her nursing home bed. When she had breathed her last, there was a sense of relief—for her as well as for us. We shed our tears in the corridor outside her room and comforted each other that when we saw her again, she would be in her prime, even more than fully restored—transformed—in her resurrection body.

What we are told in the gospels about Jesus' resurrection body, is in fact, the biggest reason for us to be advocates for the body. There are various ancient stories of other "gods" who disguised themselves as humans to see what was going on earth below. But the stories always describe the gods scurrying back up to their place of abode after only a cursory look around. None took on human bodily form, or lived openly among people, or died and returned to life again. And none kept their body for eternity. Only Jesus. He came in human flesh to join us—his creations of flesh and blood.

When he appeared after his resurrection, Jesus made sure that his disciples experienced his physical presence with them. He ate with them and invited them to touch him. Though he was forever changed, he was not a ghost. Moreover, he did not just disappear at the end of his forty days preparing his disciples for their mission. They saw him bodily ascend into the sky to continue his cosmic rule as the God-man, and they were promised he would return in the same way. In some wonderful sense, he became like us so that we can become like him.

JESUS' RESURRECTION IS FOR US

For this reason, we can assert with confidence that Jesus' bodily resurrection is endorsement of our human body. It is the indicator, the first pickings of grain or fruit, showing what is to come at the harvest, at the climax of time. It also tells us that the body is not something to be got out of the way (by asceticism or death) so that we can find complete freedom and spiritual expression as an ethereal being. The resurrection very strongly affirms that we are clearly more than the sum of molecules that die, but that we will experience continuing bodily existence as unique individuals. This is much superior to immortality of the soul or dissolving into a universal "principle."

Our body, both now, and then, is part of our totality as body-persons. Through it we relate to one another, to the spiritual realm and to God who is spirit. Sometimes the Bible uses the word *soul* to speak of the total human person—body and mind, consciousness and will, physical breath and spirit. Biblical language is not precise on this, but the clear emphasis is always on wholeness, integration, and the totality of the person in relation to themselves, others and God.

In writing about what we will become in life after life, the Apostle Paul uses the analogy of the relationship of the seed to the plant to which it gives life (1 Cor 15). When a wheat grain falls into the ground and apparently dies, its new life is as a wheat plant, not a eucalypt! It has wheat DNA with all the promise for new wheat life. In the same way, there is change of bodily form in our resurrection, but continuity of who we are. Our body is essential to our human identity, it is part of our total makeup and so continues after death, in a new form.

Moreover, our certain prospect of resurrection should inform, not only how we think about death, but also change how we live here and now, and how we take care of our bodies. In 1 Corinthians 6, Paul asserts that our coming resurrection gives us the motive for right living (including sexual morality) because we should not treat our bodies badly, knowing we are people linked to Christ and destined to be like him. Resurrection people.

Of course, the Christian hope of life beyond death in a resurrection body does not avoid the hard slog of earthly existence, nor the harsh reality of our own or a loved one's death, but it is an affirmation of bodily life here and now. For women, whose bodies have either been admired, worshipped, or alternatively, rubbished as things to be used, it is doubly important to value how God has created us.

THE WONDER OF BEING BODY-PERSONS

Christians, therefore, are advocates for the body, especially women's bodies! It almost sounds like heresy! For while Jesus did not seem to have problems being a body-person, there has always been an ascetic stream in Christian thinking. Saint Francis, for example, called the body, "Brother Ass." Original sin and on-going temptation, he said, were to be fought by suppressing the appetites of the body, the enemy. Margaret Miles calls this asceticism at its extreme, the "rape of the body for the good of the soul" and identifies the same disregard for the body in negative habits such as working excessively, overeating, drug use, promiscuity and pornography.[5] N.T. Wright reminds us that this separation of the spirit from the body, resurgent in western thinking of the last two hundred years, has its origins in Greek Platonic thought, not Christian thinking.[6]

Sometimes, Christians devalue the body because they say the Apostle Paul implies in his letters to first-century churches that "flesh" is a bad thing. But this is a misunderstanding of "flesh." We can see from the context that sometimes by *flesh* he just means the physical body and there is no condemnation. For example, in his longest discussion of the resurrection when he is speaking about our physical bodies and what God has in mind for them, he refers to all bodies, animal and human ones, as *flesh* (1 Cor 15:39). In another place when he is warning about spiritual opposition, he says it does

---

5. Miles, *Fulness of Life*, 16.

6. Wright makes a strong case in *Surprised by Hope* for the damaging influence of Plato regarding life after death in western thought.

not come from us flesh and blood people, but from the spiritual powers that oppose us (Eph 6:12).

At other times, however, Paul contrasts *flesh* with *Spirit*[7], that is, the Holy Spirit (Gal 5:16–21; Rom 8:3–9). There he is speaking of people pursuing a way of living that is self-absorbed, relying only on their personal resources and opposed to God. *Flesh* in this context is sensuality, but not only that—it is a whole way of life lived in pursuit of oneself and definitely not what God wants for us. Paul is urging his hearers to make a lifestyle choice—do not live as if only the physical flesh matters but live in step with the Holy Spirit. Both God's design for living and the selfish path, take place *in* the body. "The body is a prize that the spirit and the flesh must struggle to possess," declares Miles, using flesh in this second sense—of self-seeking life.[8]

Dallas Willard describes the value and importance of the body to the human spirit this way, "Put simply—no body, no power. People have a body for one reason—that we might have at our disposal the resources that would allow us to be persons in fellowship and cooperation with a personal God."[9] The promise is that our body can, through openness to God's Spirit, express the wholeness that Jesus brings. Willard in a later book goes on to describe the body as the "power pack" of our spirit. "The body is the focal point of our presence in the physical and social world. In union with it, we come into existence and become the persons we shall forever be. The body is our primary energy source or 'strength'—our personalized 'power pack.'"[10]

This is a very positive and practical understanding of the connection between our human flesh and our self in relation to God. We cannot be spiritual without expressing it through our body. So let us value the physical body!

CARING FOR OUR BODIES

Christian advocacy for the body means taking seriously, right now, how we live with these wonderful *power packs* God has given us, bringing them into top condition when possible as expressions of the Creator's handiwork, and as instruments of service to others. We do this by healthy living, including exercise and rest, and good mental health.

---

7. Translators add the capital to "Spirit" to make it clear that the Holy Spirit is referred to.
8. Miles, *Fulness of Life*, 158.
9. Willard, *Spirit of the Disciplines*, 92.
10. Willard, *Renovation of the Heart*, Loc. 402, Kindle.

Caring for our body also includes spiritual practices such as solitude and prayer which enable us to stand back and hear the necessary correctives among the everyday demands of the "rat race." People associate spiritual disciplines with abstaining from things and activities. In some areas of life, abstinence is called for to make way for something better, but we should also be pursuing spiritual disciplines to maximize our engagement with life itself. These disciplines will be like the ones athletes need in preparing for competition—skills development, peak fitness and the mental readiness to produce a top performance through our body every time.

I am aware that this is an ideal not all can attain. Some are born with deficits they must accept. Others acquire them through quirks of their chromosomes, susceptibility to infections or accidents. All of us eventually get old. Certainly, our bodies can give us a lot of pain, but even in the midst of it, affirming our bodies as basically good, helps us respond appropriately when they are disabled or malfunction. Suffering goes with being human. It does matter and cannot be dismissed as good for the soul (the old asceticism) or a deserved result of a person's karma because of the way they have lived (New Age thinking). If we understand the body to be an integral part of our person, then caring for ourselves should be very intentional and practical. And like Jesus in his healing ministry, we offer that care to others.

Jesus often uses what happens to us to teach us new things and draw us into a deeper relationship, but he does not relish seeing a person in pain, any more than we would. His commitment to healing is prominent in the gospel record, and compassion for the hungry and the thirsty has always characterised the best of Christian involvement. Indeed, compassion for others is a more constructive corrective to our tendency to self-absorption, and much better than self-denial as an end in itself. In times of widespread illness or natural disaster, in plague or pandemic or earthquake, the true Christian response has always been, as N.T. Wright points out in his book on the coronavirus pandemic, helping those most affected, even at risk to ourselves.[11]

There is much more that could be said about caring for our bodies, about pain and suffering, and empathy and compassion for others, because thinking about our bodies is more than abstract philosophy. The focus here, however, is on understanding who we are as persons, and especially how that affects our everyday lives and the choices we can make. I want to give just two examples of this, both of which illustrate the connection between the physical and the spiritual.

---

11. Wright, *God and the Pandemic*.

WHAT OF THE BODY AND HUMAN SEXUALITY?

Human emotions are powerful, none more so that the push and pull of sexual drive and attraction—bodily responses very easily taking us in a harmful direction. If Christians are advocates for the body, what do we say about sexuality, one of the fundamental elements of being human? There is no doubt in Genesis 2 about the positive expression of the man-woman relationship—before our forebears' rebellion against their Creator. But equally, the Scriptures give us many examples of the consequences of sin afterwards, starting with the break in relationship between the pair in the Garden of Eden as they launch into blaming each other. There are many instances in the Bible narrative of sex used to trap or exploit people, including in the worship of other gods. One negative response by Christians to this perceived danger, has been to fear sexual activity or ban it altogether, praising those who take a life-long vow of chastity. Presumably, part of the reason why women are denigrated is that their gender has come to be associated with this distorted view of sexual activity. Thinking about our bodies as we are doing in this chapter, is therefore part of appreciating what the Creator has in mind for us *through* our bodies.

In this less than perfect world, how we think about our sexuality is a good indicator of our attitude to our body. Nowhere is this more apparent than in the way Christians read the Song of Songs—the exquisite love story in the centre of the Old Testament. For many of us, the Song is an enigma. Snatches have found their way into our wedding ceremonies as well as into our songs about God. We may even have wallowed in its poetry when we were young and first in love. But we often do not know what to make of its explicit endorsement of human beauty and sexuality, and so, when we are uncomfortable about our bodies, we quickly apply it to our relationship with God, and only to that relationship.

We need to read Song of Songs and its straight-forward attitude to human sexuality today more than ever. Western societies are devaluing marriage yet making an idol of sex; people are longing for the stability of commitment but finding it hard to commit themselves; and personal independence has become more important than mutuality and trust. The church has often reacted to a sex-soaked culture by not speaking positively about the body or about sex, not helping people appreciate the good gifts God gives us to enjoy. But here in the Song is a wonderful endorsement of the human body and love, beauty, commitment, and security—all in the context of personal faithfulness and community support. It can give us the concepts, if not the contemporary language, to present positively what others despoil. It sets us on the path, however tentatively, of exploring in our world the connection between spirituality and sexuality, the connection between body and spirit.

Those not comfortable with the Bible speaking positively about the human body, gratefully read the Song of Songs as allegory without any reference to its historical context; or as typology, identifying its characters with New Testament teaching; or as a drama, a script intended to be acted or sung at a royal wedding pageant. Observant Jews read it aloud in its entirety during Passover celebrations because they apply it to the nation of Israel as God's bride. Indeed, the book of Revelation calls the church the Bride of Christ. But have you ever heard the man's and the Song of Songs woman's fulsome descriptions of physical beauty read publicly in your church to celebrate our being the Bride of Christ? We are too embarrassed about the human body to do that!

Of course, the relationship between the two lovers can also illustrate the relationship between Christ and the believer, or between Christ and the church. But if we are to overcome our reluctance to address the issues of our bodies and of sexuality in our day, at whatever stage of life we find ourselves, we must first hear the poems speak to us as people made in the image of the God who is the very essence of relationship. They amplify the physicality of the wonderful male-female relationship and marriage as described in Genesis 2.

I encourage you to read the Song of Songs again carefully and enjoy what it says about human beauty and sexual attraction and apply it to yourself. As in a good romantic novel, you will find in each of its six cycles, yearnings for love, tension and frustration, affirmations of praise and beauty, and movement towards intimacy. Surprisingly, coming from a patriarchal society, the Song has many more words in the mouth of the woman than the man. She takes the initiative in their relationship as much as he. Both are lovers, both beloved. The reciprocity of their relationship, its ups and downs, its progression over time, the call to faithfulness, the bodily enjoyment of each other, are all a wonderful endorsement of being whole body people. And a model for us.

RESPECTING OUR BODY THROUGH SLEEP[12]

The act of sleeping is a second illustration of the connection between our body and spirituality.[13] We can think of sleep as both a gift from God, and as

---

12. My writing on sleep first appeared in Turner, "Theology of Everyday Life," 212–217.

13. Banks, *Redeeming the Routines,* 15–16, first drew my attention to this aspect of

a spiritual discipline. Sleep, or the lack of it, profoundly affects us every day. It is an example of an ordinary routine—a gift—given to us for our good by the Creator of our body. Yet to receive this gift requires our cooperation, because many of us constantly try to skip sleep or make do with less of it in order to fit more things into our lives.

Studies show that in western societies, most urban dwellers are chronically sleep-deprived. Lack of sleep gives rise to fraught relationships, precipitates or exacerbates depression, causes us to perform less effectively and to make poor decisions. Researchers continue to uncover more and more functions of the body that require sleep's hiatus of activity, particularly in the dark hours, to do their job and re-set for the next day. The list of functions renewed by sleep includes heart, blood vessels, kidneys, muscles, the immune system, and growth. In the brain, sleep allows reorganisation of memory and other tasks, and promotes plasticity and of course, learning.

At eight hours a night if we live to seventy years, we should be spending more than twenty-three of them in sleep—necessary for our body, but something most of us resent as a waste of time. Eager to get on with work or study or leisure, we constantly look for ways to make do with less than is good for us. This is not taking appropriate care of our bodies or recognising the connection between our body and our spiritual life. There is no sense in depriving our body of needed sleep. In fact, regularly foregoing sleep may be willful disregard of the Creator's exquisite plan for us.

SLEEP AND THE DISCIPLINE OF ABSTINENCE

Willard, in his foundational work on spiritual formation mentioned previously, makes a helpful distinction between disciplines of *abstinence* and disciplines of *engagement*.[14] Sleep as a discipline falls into both categories. Like fasting, we may choose to *abstain* from sleep, forgoing a good for something better. We may abstain, for example, in order to watch and pray—maintain a vigil. That is what Jesus asked of his disciples when he agonized on the Mount of Olives the night before his crucifixion. Similarly, staying awake to sit with a friend or family member in distress, may be a discipline of abstinence, a costly act of love.

Newborn babies seem to delight in arriving after dark. My experience of multiple night-time labors, sacrificing sleep for my coming child, was a worthwhile sacrifice, though I suspect it was also preparation for the weeks of night feeds that were to follow—night feeds that seemed to go on forever!

---

the theology of everyday life.

14. Willard, *Spirit of the Disciplines*, 158.

Of course, both giving birth and frequent feeds were sleep forgone in a good cause! But I did not want to continue the sleep deprivation indefinitely.

Jesus expressed disappointment at the failure of his disciples to watch with him that betrayal night. When I conduct a retreat, I see many people fighting sleep, because sleeping feels like failure or at least a lack of devotion—the enemy of spirituality. Yet on a longer retreat, a short nap can be a useful first step into solitude and silence—a precursor to hearing from God. But in today's busy world, sleepiness can also be a signal to stop and reassess how we are living. A better routine of going to bed earlier may be all that is necessary. When extended quiet or prayer repeatedly slides into sleep, however, deeper medical or spiritual issues may warrant exploration.

SLEEP IS A SIGN OF TRUSTING GOD

Choosing to be disciplined about getting sufficient rest on a regular basis means sleep is also a discipline of *engagement*—a commitment to live how God intends in these *power packs* of ours. Resting in God is an act of humility, an expression of our creatureliness, acknowledging that all we desire, all we are working towards, does not depend on us. The universe will continue even if we are asleep! We are giving up any pretension to being in charge, in deference to the God who reigns.

In one of his kingdom parables, Jesus points to the farmer planting his crop. Whether he sleeps or works, the crop grows without his help until it is ready, and the grain can be reaped (Mark 4:26–29). We are like that farmer. We do not control our world. Only God does. The message is that it is God who is bringing in the kingdom, and although we are invited to participate, God is the one doing the work of growing the seed. Jesus follows these words with a parable of a mustard seed growing to a great bush, using, as he often does, a repetition of his significant teaching to give it emphasis. He reiterates—any growth, but particularly Kingdom growth—is in God's hands, not ours. It happens even when we sleep.

This trusting God to work while we are asleep is deeply counter-cultural in our western societies. We assume our strenuous effort will get us results, and we measure our worth by how much we achieve, how much we pack into our life, and how busy we are. But if we lie down at night with a prayer of gratitude for the day, if we let go and let God run the universe while we sleep, this is a wonderful expression of trust and engagement with our Creator, as well as respect for the bodily people we are.

We are not naked spirits, now or in the hereafter. The resurrection affirms the continuing importance of the human body and the connection between our body and our spirit. We cooperate in our body with the work of the Holy Spirit. This is honoring to the one who created us, and to the Spirit who is remaking us. By building adequate sleep into our daily routine, we are better fitted to serve God in this world.

Of course, there are times when for medical reasons or season of life, dropping off to sleep or getting enough sleep is not easy. But the fundamental principle is that God made us need sleep for our physical strength to be renewed and our brains to do their processing work. Getting enough sleep is an act of appreciation and worship of the one who gave us our bodies.

THINK ABOUT THESE THINGS

The Apostle Paul reminded the Christians in Philippi to think about the true, noble, lovely things God has made (Phil 4:8). That includes our human body. It is wonderfully made. But valuing it has not always been part of Christian culture, nor have we seen how our coming resurrection should influence the daily treatment of these wonderful *power packs* God has created.

Jesus was realistic about human bodily misuse and rebellion, yet he embraced his body, gave it for us in life and death, and continues to identify with us and minister to us. By the Holy Spirit and our cooperation, he promises us a better way to live. As we appreciate the Creator's handiwork, we invite the Holy Spirit's transforming power to develop beauty of character in our disciplined bodies, given in the service of others.[15]

Personal Reflection

> "With your very own hands you formed me:
> now breathe your wisdom over me so I can understand you"
> (Ps 119:73 The Message).

> "For you [Lord] you created my inmost being;
> you knit me together in my mother's womb.
> I praise you because I am fearfully and wonderfully made;
> your works are wonderful, I know that full well" (Ps 139:13–14).

We are indeed "wonderfully made." Reflect on the miracle and the mystery of the human body. Look at your hands, your face. Laugh, sing, dance. Ponder what you appreciate most in your own body and what it can do. Thank your Creator for it.

---

15. Some material in this chapter first appeared in Turner, "Let's Get Physical."

What comfort do you take from realizing God has known you from your beginning?

How does knowing your body is the "power pack" of your spirit influence your behaviour and your habits?

Is getting good sleep a problem for you? Do you know what is causing that? Have you explored sources of advice on sleep hygiene? Do you think trusting God to run the world through the night is your issue?

7

Beautiful with God's Beauty

Good morning!
You're beautiful with God's beauty,
Beautiful inside and out!
God be with you.

—The angel Gabriel to Mary, coming to ask her to be the mother of Jesus (Luke 1:28 The Message).

IT WAS NOT SURPRISING that Mary was startled by the unexpected angelic visit, wondering what was behind a greeting like that. When she is asked if she will consent to be mother to the promised God-man, it must have been even more startling to think of herself, just an ordinary young woman, worthy of God's favor and trust. She expresses this surprise and wonder later in her song of celebration at Elizabeth's house:

> *God took one good look at me, and look what happened–*
> *I'm the most fortunate woman on earth!*
> *What God has done for me will never be forgotten,*
> *the God whose very name is holy,*
> *set apart from all others.*
> *His mercy flows in wave after wave*
> *on those who are in awe before him* (Luke 1:48–50 The Message).

Mary's song reveals a life lived in awe of God. That is what made her beautiful, inside and out. She was beautiful in devotion and spiritual awareness; personality and generosity too, perhaps, but very aware that the kind of beauty that prepared her for the God-bearing task was itself a grace gift from God. The expression used by the angel and translated "beautiful" in The Message paraphrase, and "highly favored" in many other translations, comes from the word for grace—something given by God freely but undeservedly. Probably like most of us, Mary had experienced awe at God's creation of the natural world and its powerful motivating emotion which leads us to worship the Creator. But now she is deeply in awe of personally receiving God's favor. Her "yes" to accepting this invitation to be the mother of Jesus, shows she had confidence that what God asked of her, God would make possible.

SEEING OUR BEAUTY AS OUR CREATOR SEES IT

This book encourages you to see yourself as your Creator sees you, with all your potential. In the previous chapter, we considered our attitude to our physical bodies, but here we must address more specifically the beauty of being a woman. Like the flowers we admire or the scenery that takes our breath away, beauty of face or figure is also a God-given gift, though one rarely spoken of favorably by Christians, because we fear being defined by our looks. Yet, created by a good God, accepted in Jesus and given the Holy Spirit as our constant companion, we should be able to walk through this world with an inner confidence that is reflected in feeling comfortable in our own skin.

I find few who write about being a disciple of Jesus have a positive understanding of human beauty, and especially women's beauty. Some urge us to teach our daughters they are princesses, daughters of the King of kings, but that evokes an image of pretty dresses and leisured poses, which is a rather narrow perspective on women's strength and agency. Others encourage us to make the most of ourselves for our husbands—a worthwhile expression of love, but again a diminished and instrumental understanding of female beauty. Writers who do address the subject of beauty from a Christian perspective usually major on warnings about the vanity of excessive self-regard, or the danger of massaging our body image for public display. In the interests of thrift or the environment, others may caution against unnecessary expenditure on beauty products or clothing. There is little support for Christian women to think positively about their beauty. An article by Australian Jenny Denny is provocatively titled, *If God doesn't hate my body, why should I?* It thoughtfully approaches the topic from her lived experience of a harmful negative body image. She claims she could only find three Christian books[1] which even in part discuss how a woman should regard her body's attractiveness.

In a dearth of positive understanding of human beauty, this chapter approaches the topic from a number of perspectives, starting with awe at God's creation. That creation includes the beauty of the human body. Then secondly, because the common assumption is that being human is to be overtaken by sin, I ask the question: What difference does it make that we are invited to be new creations in Christ, beautiful inside and out?

THE POWER OF AWE

I live by the Indian Ocean. It is a great gift for which I am daily thankful. The restless sea is different every wind and tide, the sunsets can be brilliant and the sea breezes very welcome in our relentless summer. Even winter storms have their beauty as well as their power. And just occasionally, there are dolphins swimming past as a bonus. Delight at the beauty of the natural world seems like an echo of God's—our thoughts and emotions having their impetus in the Creator of all these things.

In times of feeling powerless or distressed, many have found solace in looking out and up in awe at God's creation. A year ago during the first lockdown in our city caused by the Covid-19 pandemic, some of our neighbours were feeling the constrictions and loneliness of isolation. So we started meeting each night at sunset on our lawn, and social distancing, watched the sun go down over the nearby ocean. In awe of the colors, we enjoyed its beauty together, and valued our connection to each other. Later as the days got shorter and colder, and standing on the front lawn was not so inviting, we took photos of sunsets and sunrises and sent them to each other online.

Awe is an interesting word. Definitions of it often wrestle with its negative side—fear and powerlessness. Yet wonder at something bigger and more potent than ourselves is what gives awe its restorative properties. It stimulates positive emotions and in times of loss, provides a renewed perspective on our personal condition. We may be little and weak, but God goes on ordering the world as the sun rises and sets, the moon follows its path, and the seasons roll on.

Fuller Seminary's Thrive Center investigates positive psychological approaches especially for young people and completed research which

---

1. Anna McGahan's *Metanoia*; Michelle Graham's *Wanting to be her*; and Tim Keller's *The Freedom of Self-forgetfulness*.

demonstrates that experiencing natural wonder is one of the best resources available to reduce teenage depression. Specifically, being in nature can measurably diminish feelings of impatience and aggression, and stimulate generosity.[2] Even when the person cannot get out into the environment, shared photographs of awe-inspiring scenery provoke valuable memories of past beauty and arouse wonder and gratefulness all over again.

GIVING THANKS WHERE THANKS IS DUE

The majesty of sky and sea, of sun, moon and stars, are so far beyond anything we humans can construct with all our technology, it is no wonder that people have long worshipped nature. On a visit to Machu Picchu in Peru a few years ago, my husband and I spent two days exploring the ancient Inca site and observed how its orientation was chosen so the royal priests could lead worship of the rising sun in the east at dawn. On the second day, getting up very early with our tour group, we experienced the first rays of light appearing through what were once the temple windows. It was majestic and warming. The guide formed our group into a circle and led a prayer of thanks to the sun and mother earth, just as the long-gone Inca priests had done each morning. My thoughts turned instead to the Creator of the universe, and I was filled with awe at this evidence of God's handiwork. And gave thanks.

That dawn, like a first Eden, also reminded me that, as wonderful and magnificent is the physical world, people are the pinnacle of God's creation. At the highpoint of the creation story in Genesis 1, the man and the woman are created to inhabit this wonderful world, and the narrator pronounces: "God saw all that he had made, and it was very good" (Gen 1:31). Not just *good* like the first elements of creation—but *very* good.

We delighted in each of our sons at their birth. As do most parents, we gazed into our baby's little face, counted his fingers and toes, and looked for family likeness. Such miracles, such potential, wrapped up in a tiny human bundle! Our hearts sang among the pain and messiness of giving birth and our response each time to the miracle of human life seemed like the Creator's—a glimpse of God's pleasure at this new person, made beautiful, wonderful, in the divine image.

---

2. Mangan, https://www.thethrivecenter.org/finding-awe-in-uncertain-times

GOD CREATED HUMAN BEAUTY BUT IS IT DANGEROUS?

We will consider later the beauty of character the Holy Spirit brings to our lives, but first, we must focus on physical beauty because it is often dismissed or ignored. Why are we so reluctant to celebrate physical attributes? Why can we not appreciate another's beauty as God's creation too? We enjoy beauty in nature, and we appreciate the miracle of a baby. We read of both a woman's and a man's attractiveness in the Bible's Song of Songs. In that love story, one of the delights is the woman's open expression and celebration of her physical beauty. "I am a rose of Sharon, a lily of the valleys," she sings (Song 2:1).

I suspect that one reason many are reluctant to celebrate female beauty, is that women as well as men are afraid of the power of beauty displayed in a woman's body. It can be confronting, unsettling, even threatening to our understanding of modesty when the physical body is noticed or lauded. We wonder if acknowledging someone's beauty will distant them from us as an object, not a person. And of course, as relationship people made in the likeness of the relationship God, that should be our highest concern.

Women are also concerned about the possibility of being discounted, even exploited for their beauty. We have had a public conversation in Australia at various times about the nude in classic painting. The nude pose suggests that a woman is only beautiful when she is passive—an available object of desire whose worth is centred in her external beauty. This narrow conception of womanhood is rightly rejected by those who value the vigor and intellect of women as well.

THE MALE GAZE

The tenor of our times has turned this discussion towards the danger of the male gaze, suggesting the power imbalance it exemplifies will only encourage more male violence towards women. What is the connection between the display of the female body and abusive male power? Is it dangerous to display beauty? Is it threatening to women to be the object of the gaze? And where does responsibility lie when a man cannot control his desire to possess beauty innocently displayed? This danger to the woman (and to the man) is not solved by hiding or downplaying a woman's beauty. In some cultural or religious settings, this fear of the body leads to totally covering the woman's beauty to all except her husband. But beauty hidden away is beauty lost, just as if, when sun or moon are worshipped, we refuse to acknowledge how beautiful they are.

An unsettling response to a women's beauty displayed in the public space was recently generated in Australia by a photo posted on network social media of Tayla Harris, a female Australian football player, in the act of high kicking a goal. It is a beautiful and powerful depiction of a woman energetically engaging in what was until only recently, a sport that was the sole prerogative of men. For that reason, but perhaps also because it was photographed from below at a revealing angle, the network website was swamped by misogynistic trolls. So they took the image down.

Widespread protests greeted this retreat, and the network was forced to restore the photo and apologize for their action in removing it, conceding that its removal disempowered women. The image has since been made into a bronze statue and displayed in the centre of Melbourne as a celebration of female athletes. However, the incident suggests there is still something confronting to the general community about women's beauty and athleticism.

In answer to this ambivalence about women's beauty—our own or another's—I want to suggest some approaches for us to celebrate human beauty as God intended.

ADMIRING WITHOUT POSSESSING

I remember one day wading along a nearby beach with my granddaughter, hunting for shells. Just as fossickers have done for generations, she picked up the beautiful ones, ready to take them home. This time, however, I was convicted about this impetus to possess and so suggested she leave them there for others to enjoy. I knew that once home, the shells would soon be abandoned, hidden away, or thrown out. Fortunately, we cannot sequester the beauty of a sunset or a surging tide, though people have been known to cage birds to admire their plumage and song! In the natural landscape of Western Australia where I live, late winter and spring bring a wonderful display of wildflowers to our botanical hotspot. Their natural beauty is unique and the temptation to pick them very strong. Only laws forbidding it ensure they are left for others to enjoy.

So firstly, can we learn to admire without possessing? Can we appreciate beauty without trying to grab it for ourselves? Or when we see beauty in another woman, can we enjoy it without envying it or thinking we deserve to have it too? I realise that when I look at the young women I know, I admire their freshness, their taut skin, their unaffected glow of goodness, and sometimes I am jealous that it is no longer mine.

BEING COMFORTABLE IN OUR OWN SKIN

Secondly, can we learn to be comfortable in our own skin? In western culture many ways are offered to build self-esteem. Daily affirmations and positive thinking may help in the way that cognitive behaviour therapy can change habits of thought. Some self-boosting methods are not honoring of others, however. For example, comparing ourselves favorably to someone who ranks lower than us, or has faults that we do not have, may make us feel better for a short time but is not respectful to them. Developing competence in dressing and makeup, can contribute to feeling comfortable in our own skin. But rather than seeking to simply raise our self-esteem, a better and healthier attitude to *self* would be *self-acceptance*—the absence of self-hate.[3]

All of us have some desirable characteristics—personality and character, hopefully—but also elements of physical beauty. If we accept our particular allotment of physical assets, maximize them by healthy living and competent handling of our self, we can then relax into God's delight as an adored daughter. And within the bounds of modesty and wise expenditure, we can let others delight in us too as we grow in confidence to present our self to the world.

This applies to all the facets of being a woman, not just to beauty. As we saw in the introduction, Benner encourages us to pursue *deep knowing* of our self as a necessary step on our way to deep knowing of God.[4] Deep knowing of self includes understanding and appreciating our body and learning to be comfortable in being made in the image of the Creator and home to the Holy Spirit.

Having a poor body image is probably more common for women than men. But whether we are female or male, it is made worse by our culture's growing habit of sharing posed or perfected images on social media, by cat-walk presentations of glamorous models, and the spreading use of pornography. None of us is a perfect specimen, even if we try to pretend so by photoshopping our Instagram image. Psychologist Arch Hart suggests that one danger of the emerging social-media technologies is that they increase *self-consciousness*, and this is replacing *self-awareness*.[5] Self-consciousness is the opposite of being comfortable in our own skin. By excessively focusing attention on our self, we will always come up short, leading to dissatisfaction and envy.

---

3. Hart, *Me, Myself, and I*, 54.
4. Benner, *Gift of Being Yourself,* 53.
5. Hart, *Me, Myself, and I,* 105.

Some people suffering excessive self-consciousness hide themselves away from all meaningful relationships, afraid of rejection. Alternatively, others grasp every opportunity to sell themselves to the highest bidder and try to establish their personal worth through another's eyes. Both responses suggest the presence of *shame*—a burden many women carry that contributes to their negative view of their body as well as their personhood. Shame is an important and relevant topic in this discussion, but we will discuss it specifically in the next chapter.

VALUING SELF-AWARENESS

So what is lost when self-consciousness replaces self-awareness? As we have seen in the many dimensions of the self we have discussed in this book, self-awareness is good and necessary for a godly understanding of our potential. Self-awareness also helps us see how we affect others and how they are responding to us. When we are comfortable with who God has made us, we can accept what is less than perfect and relax into relationships with our family, friends, and our self. We can even sift through feedback and criticism to hear what is useful and let that inform our choices and our life goals.

So how can we enjoy the beauty of being a woman with a healthy self-awareness that does not cringe at our defects? And how do we revel in our uniqueness without crying that our nose is too big, or our feet too small or we wish we were a bit taller or our hair more manageable? I can testify that getting older can make us even more critical of our body deficiencies as gravity has its way! But aging also brings with it a perspective about what is most important—relationships, care for others, responsibility for the created world. We also put comfort higher up the list! Stilettos have long been forsaken!

It helps to remember that the characteristics considered beautiful in a woman vary from culture to culture and with each generation. What beauty looks like in a woman in Australia or America is different from Africa or China, although less than it used to before the globalisation of our images, and western dress became almost universal. Hopefully, however, we can still appreciate the God-given variety of physical and national and gender differences and celebrate those differences. Generous variety is a theme of the natural world.

SELF-ACCEPTANCE IS MORE DIFFICULT FOR SOME

To this chapter's endorsement of valuing our physical appearance, I want to express a reservation, however. Even with all the beauty training, careful grooming and artistic choice of clothing and comfort in being a woman in all its dimensions, we dare not rely on our own efforts to generate self-acceptance. This is doubly true for those whose life has been battered by harsh experience or rejection and who find themselves abandoned by those whom they naturally expect to love them unconditionally—parents, chosen partner, children. It is not surprising that women who have experienced such treatment find it hard to think positively about themselves. They carry a particularly heavy legacy.

There are approaches which can walk a woman through to healing of these extraordinary hurts. I have had the privilege of convening programs of restoration alongside psychotherapy professionals. I have also seen people gifted in focused prayer have an effective ministry to battered and bruised women. God has brought recovery and self-acceptance to many, including among my friends, family, and church. The common ground for all such therapies is a process of acknowledging the hurts, bringing them to Jesus the great healer, and entering into the grace of God's and their own self-acceptance. With a lot of prayer and practical support.

This is not waving a magic wand. Generally, it requires the woman to undertake prolonged personal work. The damage to the core of her being can be deep and strongly protected, and a restored life is not realised immediately. Recovery includes growing new habits of thinking and ways of living with the encouragement of others. But just as we all are called to welcome the Holy Spirit's power, daily forming us into the image of Christ, so the Spirit goes on working in God's damaged children to restore the health and joy the Creator intended at the beginning.

CELEBRATING BEAUTY THROUGH THE CLOTHES WE WEAR

A third approach to celebrating our beauty as women is to see decisions about what we wear as positive affirmations of human beauty. One Australian style writer recently urged all women to ditch their black clothes worn as a sign of sophistication (or to hide body faults) and add some color to the world by a least a bright belt or a contrasting shade. It has made me think about whether what I wear brings joy to others as well as to myself and my Creator. Clothes clearly have a utilitarian value. We dress for both comfort and modesty. But do we also dress to enhance and display God-given beauty? Surely this is a positive action, like arranging flowers in a vase to enjoy them inside the house, or constructing a garden using aspect and slopes to maximize its natural growth and beauty.

This includes acknowledging, however, that we do dress to hide our body "faults." What we hide, or highlight, is of course conditioned by culture and generation and is not necessarily negative. Through choice of garments and colors and style we can express beauty in personality and form and make the most of what we have been given. Yet to write this way feels uncomfortable. Each morning as I dress to look my appropriate best, what am I trying to achieve? I want to affirm beauty, but I also want to avoid a hypocrisy that puts emphasis on less important things. Am I acting in faith or sin? I want above all to walk openly and rightly with my God and the people around me.

Larry Crabb, in describing sin in psychological terms, suggests self-protection is the ultimate human rebellion because it comes from not trusting God, preferring our own survival efforts rather than accepting God's generosity. Sin makes us ashamed to stand naked spiritually before God, yet we know that nakedness is necessary to receive grace. The rebelling man and woman in the first garden, aware of their nakedness, tried covering up in fig leaves but it was not enough. God's enough—the promise of redemption through Jesus—was the answer symbolized by the gift of a covering of skins. In Benner's words, "Complete knowing of our self in relation to God includes three things: our self as deeply loved, our self as deeply sinful, and our self as in a process of being redeemed and restored."[6] Clothes used as a form of self-protection are a poor substitute for knowing we are acceptable to God but deriding or hiding the physical beauty given to us is not God-glorifying either.

RESISTING BEAUTY CONSUMERISM

This points us to another topic linked to the beauty business: the incessant pressure on women to spend excessive time and money to make themselves beautiful—on cosmetics, treatments, surgery, as well as on clothes. Much more than maximizing the assets God has given, this compulsive chasing after beauty may have its genesis in a woman feeling she is only acceptable wearing a mask, not in revealing her real self.

---

6. Benner, *Gift of Being Yourself,* 67.

How much is excessive time and money? Legalism has had too much sway in this arena among Christians in the past, so instead of making rules I suggest some questions we can ask ourselves as we choose how to live. Am I driven by vanity, focusing more on external appearance than on qualities of character? Am I spending more money on beauty products than on worthwhile causes I know are more important? Can I be metaphorically naked before others? Do I think my worth depends on others' admiration? Does my desire for perfect beauty make me unavailable or passive, like a reclining portrait, rather than a pilgrim grasping with both hands the call to follow that Jesus issues to his disciples? Can I put into my contemporary context the Apostle Peter's guidance, "Your beauty should not come from outward adornment, such as elaborate hairstyles and wearing of gold jewelry or fine clothes. Rather, it should be that of your inner self, the unfading beauty of a gentle and quiet spirit, which is of great worth in God's sight" (1 Pet 3:3–4).

We are right to be wary of being defined just by our physical attributes. The Bible, despite lauding the Creator's design for creation, is generally very cautious in promoting human beauty as an end in itself. Women described as beautiful are usually also seen in the context of their character and activity. Esther, for example, is noted as winning a beauty contest to become queen, but she is remembered most in Scripture for her courage and creativity in facing the king's displeasure as she maneuvers to protect her Hebrew people. Proverbs 31's picture of the ideal wife praises everything, from her trading, cooking, weaving, and sewing skills to her management, wisdom, and child-rearing. No passivity here, but the chapter concludes, "Charm is deceptive, and beauty is fleeting; but the woman who fears the Lord is to be praised" (Prov 31:30).

MORE THAN PRINCESSES

So how do we walk this tightrope of celebrating beauty while not defining ourselves by it? One movement already mentioned, designed to counter society's over-emphasis on external appearance, yet still acknowledge female beauty, has been promoting women as captivating princesses in the royal family of God the King. In Christian bookshops, the merchandise and advice books for this are usually in girl-pink, and the stress is on femininity, being desirable, and fulfilled in capturing and holding your man. The imagery is particularly directed at young women struggling with body image, encouraging them to feel valued and take delight in their appearance. And what girl has not longed to be rescued by Prince Charming when she feels like a Cinderella. Dissatisfaction with themselves in adolescent years is often expressed by young women, and some move on to treating their body in ways that are destructive.

Australian Anna McGahan experienced that and points us to a better way. She has written an insightful narrative of her own struggle from childhood to accept her real self. Although she became an accomplished actress, her personal loathing was manifest in her body, which she punished over many years of extravagant and abandoned living, experiencing anorexia, promiscuity, and rootlessness. Later, in a journey towards God she devoured the Scriptures and discovered the Apostle Paul's words in 1 Corinthians (6:19) reminding his hearers that their bodies are a temple for the Holy Spirit. In the wonder of that divine acceptance, she started listening to and caring for her body and it responded by setting itself right again. Thinking of her body as a sanctuary for God, she writes:

> God had made himself at home and called that home "good." I had no choice but to believe him. She was my home, too . . . For the first time in ten years, I had room to think about something other than food and exercise. I had room to find my body fascinating and attractive and complex, because I knew her, and I knew she was all those things. I had the capacity to love again.[7]

This is self-awareness and self-acceptance, both expressed beautifully in the light of God's indwelling her body.

THE REALITY OF OUR HUMAN FALLENNESS

In the previous chapter we saw that some people associate anything to do with the physical body as sinful. They picture the "spiritual" at war against the "natural" in all dimensions of life, as if we must choose one side or the other. They label something "human" or "natural," and so discount it, painting it as evil. Human beauty gets put in this category. But that is not how the Creator sees us. We have the dignity of being in God's image.

Neither did being human diminish the God-man whom Mary was asked to bring to birth. Jesus was fully human and fully God, displaying the full capacity of being human as well as the divinity of being God. It is that awareness of the value of each human person that has prompted Christians in all eras to take the lead in caring for the least of God's children.

Nevertheless, we must acknowledge the fallenness of human beings. We have noted the very good beauty of God's initial creation, but readers of Genesis know that the story does not end there. All does not stay *very good*

---

7. McGahan, *Metanoia*, 120–121.

in the garden of delights. The first people were damaged by their disobedience and damaged each other. The consequences of their sin also inflicted distress on the physical world, and it has become increasingly obvious that we twenty-first century descendants are just as careless in caring for our planet as we are of each other, and driven more by exploitation than wise use of our human dignity.

Even our homes, where understanding and mutual care should be most apparent, have become places of danger, especially for women and children. People wanting to be self-sufficient, to be equal with or ignore the Creator, have repeated through the generations that first sin of pride with the same resulting disaster, causing loss of innocence and openness, disrupting human relationships. What hope is there for restoration of that Eden perfection? And what will the Creator do about our spoiling these human works of art?

AN ORIGAMI CRANE

One of my sons is great at paper folding, origami-style. Once when I was describing to a congregation this catastrophe in the Garden of Eden, the result of the first man and woman's disobedience, I gave him a piece of glossy origami paper and asked him to make his specialty—a paper crane. When it was finished, he handed it to me, and I displayed it for all to see its handsome shape. Then I took it, scrunched it, and threw it away. People gasped. Such wanton destruction of something beautiful! So I picked up the paper crane and carefully started to press out its wrinkles and return it to the beautiful bird it was created to be. It still had the creases, the imperfections, but it was recognizably a splendid crane again. That to me is a picture of what God longs to do with the spoiled creation, if we consent to it. The Apostle Paul tells us that if anyone is in Christ, that person is a new creation (2 Cor 5:17). The transformation begins when we turn back and acknowledge God's sovereignty, but it does not happen overnight. We live in the in-between time, on the way to being restored, but we are not yet there. We will not be fully restored until we are part of the new heavens and the new earth at the end of time.

NEW CREATIONS IN CHRIST

When I am teaching in east Africa, I am sometimes asked what I think a congregation should do if a man with more than one wife becomes a Christian and joins the fellowship. The practice in many churches is to require the man to divorce the second (and any third) wife. Although the expectation is that the husband will continue to support his former wives and their children, at least financially, it often does not happen. I have discovered that the person asking me this question is usually one such second wife who has found herself and her children discarded with little means of support and no father to her children. This hardly presents the church community as a haven of care. Moreover, all those affected are not allowed to be part of the leadership of the congregation.

As an outsider to their culture, it is not my place to give advice on how such complex dilemmas can be resolved. But after hearing this concern expressed many times by abandoned wives, I asked one of my African colleagues what his answer would be. His straightforward response was that a person "in Christ" is a new creation, the old has gone. This means that both the husband and the wives should be treated as new creations and fully accepted in the congregation. Then, together with the church leaders, they can work out how best to deal with the ongoing consequences in their family of their previous life.

NEW CREATION WOMEN

All of us who have come to Christ are new creations whom God is restoring to the original creation design—into all we are meant to be. The pathway to recovery, including the wonderful potential of women and men having authentic and mutual relationships with one another, is available to all, even though many do not choose to take this journey towards Jesus.

Tim Keller tells the story of a woman who came to him for help. She had lived most of her adult life trying to find meaning and identity in a succession of dependent relations with men. She was a beautiful and successful woman and knew how to make the most of her allure to get the next, and then the next, relationship. Each time she hoped it would be the lasting one, the one to satisfy her. None did, and in her search for a better life, she found Jesus. But she had a lifetime of habits and ways of thinking that now had to be undone and replaced. She often found herself returning to seeking a man's admiration and availability to feel good about herself.

Finally, she found that when temptation came in the form of another attractive man she hoped would complete her, she was able to say, "I am a new creation. I do not need to go that path because my life is hidden with Christ in God."[8] Saying to ourselves, "I am a new creation in Christ Jesus" is an affirmation of how God sees us, and how we should regard our self.

---

8. Col 3:3. Keller, "Identity."

Unfortunately, we do not always apply that affirmation to ourselves nor to others around us.

BEAUTY OF CHARACTER FIRST

So how should we new-creation women respond to the Holy Spirit's work in us? It goes without saying that qualities of character—generosity, compassion, kindness, humility, gentleness, patience, forgiveness, and especially self-giving love—are the highest virtues that make women attractive. They are how we are designed to live and flourish in *shalom* relationship with each other as well as with God. These qualities give practical expression to what it means to be made in God's image. We invite God's Holy Spirit to restore and develop them in us to grow us into Christ's likeness, day by day.

When the Apostle Paul wrote that list of virtues in his letter to the Colossians (3:12–14) and called them fruit of the Spirit in his letter to the Galatian church (5:22–23) he applied them to all believers—men and women. They are qualities that make women beautiful, but of course we want them in the men we know too, especially in the one we are married to!

When my husband and I were celebrating our fiftieth wedding anniversary a few years ago, we were asked often what we thought made a happy marriage. We found it a difficult question but eventually came to describe the process of building our marriage as a "collaborative work of art." The expression best captures the unique creativity and mutual responsibility that is needed. The work of art did not come fully formed when we said, "I do." It took work over the years. Love, *agape* self-giving love, is of course the primary glue that binds a couple together and enables them separately and together to flourish. But sometimes *agape* love seems rather nebulous. So in our marriage, we have come to think of *kindness* as the virtue that best expresses what is needed day in, day out, in the ups and downs of life.

KINDNESS IN ALL RELATIONSHIPS

About the same time as our fiftieth wedding anniversary, an Australia Talks National Survey asked thousands of people about their lives and what they thought would make their community better. Among the 54,000 who replied, most nominated *respect* as the quality they wanted Australians to show to each other. This was distilled to a focus on being *kind* and the sponsors invited nominations through #KindnessHero! to find Australia's kindest and most compassionate people. Kindness and compassion issuing in respect for each other are indeed the qualities of character needed to build a great society (as well as a marriage).

WHAT ABOUT A RESPONSIBILITY TO BE MODEST?

There is another matter I have skirted over in this chapter that I must now address. Apart from a passing reference, I have left it to the end to discuss *modesty* because so often in the past it was seen as *the* defining issue regarding a woman displaying her beauty. Modesty is indeed a responsibility for women (and men), but it rightly comes after the discussions of self-awareness and kindness in relationships, rather than under the heading of sin or body rejection.

In today's world, the push-back in any conversation about modesty is, "Am I responsible for how another person responds to me and my God-given beauty?" and "Don't I have the right to present myself as I choose?" This is part of the larger challenge to twenty-first century western Christians—the balance between self and community, between my rights and my care for others. We live in rights-dominated societies where the balance has shifted a long way from acknowledging responsibility to care for others. We are also aware that responsibility for being modest has often asked more of women than of men.

An added difficulty is that modesty is necessarily culturally and generationally defined. I sometimes wonder if one easy way to be modest in my own culture would be to just be a decade behind the times! But that would be ignoring the issue and not helping the young women I know who want to act christianly in our society. In recent times many of us have avoided discussions about modesty because we do not want to revert to legalistic rules or be disapproving seniors. That may be abrogating responsibility!

When I go into another culture, I respect their norms and dress conservatively so as not to give offence or distract from the relationships I relish with my colleagues there. But I know they too are wrestling with how their young women are making different choices from the older generation, and they are distressed at the change that is overwhelming them, much of it coming from western societies. Avoiding the topic or simplistically adopting western rules is not helpful. More open discussion of the principles behind care for both self and community is important, there and in my own culture. But rather than jumping straight into a code of conduct, let the starting point be appreciating God-given beauty, inside and outside a woman's body. That will give delight to our Creator and to us as we appreciate what we have been given.

FOR ALL WOMEN

If you are a woman—do you delight in that? Are you grateful to the Creator who made you as you are? Are you seeing negative expectations of society about your gender overturned in your own life because you choose to believe what God says is *very good* about creation? Does your demeaner, your poise, your confidence, radiate that self-acceptance and do you teach it to your daughters and sons?

What I am suggesting in this chapter is that there is a way for all women to flourish: enjoy the beauty of person and character God has given you; guard your heart from envy and exploitation of others; and give thanks that your appreciation of God's love and your own self-acceptance can grow under the influence of the Holy Spirit so that you are beautiful inside, as well as out. This is much more empowering than thinking of yourself as a captivating princess or even a powerful athlete. It is how God intended you to be—and a gift to others.

Personal Reflection

> "You're beautiful with God's beauty,
> Beautiful inside and out!" (Luke 1:28 The Message).

The angel's words to Mary resonate down the generations. They bring to mind someone with grace, poise, at ease with herself, not so self-conscious that she cannot see another person or respond to a life challenge. And someone who lives her life with awe and gratitude to her Creator, knowing she is accepted and loved for who she is because that is the nature of our God.

What in creation most inspires awe in you?

Do you feel the same way when you see a beautiful person, even if they are very different from you?

Does being a woman bring you delight and joy?

Can you hear the angel's words addressed to you?

Can you pray—

> *O God,*
> *Help me to believe your truth about myself*
> *. . . no matter how beautiful it is!*

8

Beyond Shame

Who am I? They mock me, these lonely questions of mine.
Whoever I am, Thou knowest, O God, I am thine!
—Dietrich Bonhoeffer (1906–1945)

PUTTING YOUR HOME ON display to sell is a funny business. It is like appearing naked in public. For far too many weekends when we opened our house in Perth for sale, we had people wandering through it looking at how we lived—or appeared to live. Our books were on show—what does this family read? Our eating habits were evident. Even our sleeping arrangements, or at least what we chose to show of them, could be examined. The children felt as if they were living in a display home because no real boy would have a room as pristine as theirs was at that moment! We dared not show any dirt or signs of wear and tear. We were naked.

Preparing that house to sell (we have done it another three times since) started me pondering the relationship between openness and shame. What does one reveal and what does one hide? We painted the walls of the house to cover some superficial cracks. Presentation is everything, said the agent. We swept the leaves from the patio before an inspection to make the place look tidy and so it was not obvious that when you live under beautiful gum trees you get a lot of leaf drop! We cleaned the windows frequently because we did not want to bring to visitors' attention that living by the sea leaves you with salt on your windows after a strong blow. Was this dishonest? The theory is that the idiosyncrasies of a house are better not revealed at the falling in love stage. We acquiesced, but it was exhausting.

Afterwards, I longed to take the buyer by the hand and show them the real beauty of our home. Over the previous eleven years, we had taken a substantial but neglected house and made it beautiful. We had refinished the jarrah timber, redecorated, carpeted, and painted. The lawns were now reticulated, and the vegetable garden had compost in its sand. We built a pool for our teenage sons to use, and we were proud of our house, believing we had renovated it without being ostentatious or getting caught up in conspicuous consumption. There was a satisfaction about this kind of nakedness that I had not anticipated. Because nakedness is not only exposure, but opportunity to enjoy.

NAKEDNESS AND SHAME

I recall what was said about the first woman and man before they sinned, "Adam and his wife were both naked, and they felt no shame" (Gen 2:25). Openness without shame is a desirable thing. Being known by one's partner, without masks and props, physically and metaphorically—seen and still loved—is one of the greatest delights of marriage. It is necessary to deeply connect. A God who sees us in all our finiteness and rebellion and still loves us is an even greater and more dependable grace. Naked without pretense, yet still accepted, is great freedom, despite the vulnerability.

After the Fall, that first man and the woman were flooded by shame. Tempted, they doubted that God wanted only the best for them, and it severed their relationships. They hid from God and each other and blamed each other. We inherit their shame and wallow in our own because shame does not just slip away. In fact, in today's world, we may be even more subject to shame because the perfect individual has been made the measure of all things. As Hart says of contemporary people, "Now we have everything to hide, not just our bodies. We must hide our thoughts, because we fear we will be judged by them. We must hide our desires, because we know they will bring ridicule or rejection. We even hide our love for fear it will be rebuffed. The modern self is a self in hiding. And it hides mainly from itself."[1]

---

1. Hart, *Me, Myself, and I*, 102.

LIVING THE METAPHOR

Shame is not easy to describe, even though we know what it feels like. It needs a metaphor, like opening your house for sale. Or like giant turtles hauled up the beach and cruelly turned on their backs—helpless, exposed and with nowhere to hide.

The emotion of shame is crippling—as crippling as guilt, yet of a different hue. I first became aware of the distinction when I sat with a woman who had been a victim of incest in her childhood. She had entered a joyful relationship with God and now called herself a Christian. She knew herself to be fully accepted but could not bear to let God consciously be with her in the terrible memories of her past. "I would be too ashamed to have God see me in that place," she said. Her pain did not come from something she did. As a child she had no power against the perpetrator—it was done *to* her. We have all experienced in a lesser or greater degree the way certain smells or sounds or sights or words or dreams trigger memories of painful past events, even if they were not our doing. The shame comes from being seen in our helplessness.

But without letting our guard down, without being at least a little vulnerable, we can never enjoy the relationships we were made for. Vulnerability and its link to shame is the research specialty of Brené Brown. Her talk in 2010 on vulnerability is still one of the highest watched TED videos. She maintains that "vulnerability is the core, the heart, the center, of meaningful human experiences"[2] because our greatest fear is being unworthy of connection to other people. "Connection is why we are here," she says. We are neurologically wired to need it, but we are afraid that if people *really* see what we are like inside, they will reject us. Our greatest need—connection to others—will not be met.

A SHAMEFUL CLASS OF PEOPLE

This chapter is here in this book because, in a world where women are often ignored, or treated as second class and powerless, women experience acutely the shame of their *very being*. It may not be anything they have done or not done; it comes with the territory of their gender. But it need not be that way.

I referred in the opening chapter to the impact of a national magazine refusing to publish my description of a woman's experience, while at the same time presenting an article about a man's. This incident, still remembered 30 years later, illustrates the burden of shame that comes from

---

2. Brown, *Daring Greatly,* 12.

a rejection of our essential being. Most people asked to describe feelings of shame and vulnerability tell a story of rejection. It is the nature of shame that many of the incidents that cause pain, the exposure to yourself of yourself, or the times when you have been "caught with your pants down," might seem almost trivial, but if they touch on our being, our identity, they have a profound effect. Though the memory may linger, however, it is my testimony and that of many others, that acceptance by a significant other can take the sting out of the initial rejection.

For me, this incident of class shame came from being a woman in our society. For others, it arises from being black or poor or a single parent. The Royal Commission in Australia into Institutional Responses to Child Sexual Abuse, and the burgeoning #MeToo movement both show the value in exposing pain to public view so that others have the confidence to identify themselves with that particular experience of shame, and so seek relief. When we find others who *feel* the same hurts and shame as us, it gives us the support of recognition and solidarity. Their stories may even lead us to hope it is possible to be delivered from shame.

I do not remember anything in my childhood or upbringing that made me ashamed of being a girl but being a pioneering woman pastor brought painful rejection some years later. When I was eventually in a pastoral position, however, the pain diminished, and I discovered that my visibility had good consequences for others that I had not anticipated. Women said to me, "Because you are there, I am learning to feel better about myself. It makes a difference." Release becomes a possibility through positive identification with someone who represents us.

This is much more than tokenism. It can be seen in other spheres. When an Oscar was won some years ago by a deaf actress, many deaf people said they felt acknowledged. When a maligned cricket team from the Australian "colony" first walked all over the lads from the old mother country on their English turf, a whole nation identified with them and national self-esteem rose a few notches.

ADDRESSING SHAME THROUGH OUR RELATIONSHIP TO GOD

From the Genesis creation story, we can that see the good hunger for connection comes from being human, made in the image of the relationship God. We are meant to be in life-giving relationships with God, connected to each other, and at home in the world we were given to care for and enjoy. But now in this less than perfect world, we too often think of ourselves as helpless turtles on our backs, hiding alone in our shells, turning in shame from the God who has come to turn us right side up.

Shame is a relationship disruption and so, by its very nature, to overcome it we need outside help. We cannot just generate acceptance in our self, try as we might with multiple and frequent affirmations or self-talk. We need connection with someone who sees us differently, who rather than being over against us, identifies with us, and enters into our condition. That can begin through healthy empathetic relationships with friends and family or in skilled therapy. But it is available supremely through Jesus, who by his human life and death can represent all of us who are shamed in some way by rejection and severed relationships.

In Hart's discussion of shame, he goes on to add, "The only effective 'cure' for this shame is God's grace—God stooping to our nakedness and covering us with his own garments. The fall of Adam and Eve rendered us such a brutal blow and developed such a one-sided sense of self-consciousness in us that only restoration to God's presence, through redemption, can help remove our shame of being."[3]

THIS NECESSARY OUTSIDE HELP

This restored connection to God starts with Jesus, the God-man, in his humanness identifying with us. We are accustomed to seeing in the cross of Christ the promise of forgiveness and relief from *guilt*. Yes, Jesus pays the *penalty* for our sin. But Jesus' identification with human shame on the cross also offers the possibility of recovery from *shame*. The Roman conquerors designed crucifixion to maximize contempt and public disgrace. It was the most shameful death imaginable, carried out in a prominent place, along a well-travelled road or a hill overlooking the city. It was not a punishment ever to be applied to Roman citizens but reserved for outcasts, foreigners, and slaves. The condemned prisoner was crucified naked, bathed in bloody sweat, unable to control his excretions, even to brush away the flies. He drowned slowly as his lungs filled with fluid. To quote the Apostle Paul, Jesus' identification with us in our shame extended *even* to death on a cross (Phil 2:8, my emphasis).

Exposed there naked, his arms wide open, he embraces us and our shame so that through this death and rising from the grave we are offered a radically new self-image. The *rising* is equally as important as the martyr's death. It demonstrates Jesus' victory over the forces which demeaned him but could no longer hold him. His victory makes possible ours. Acknowledging

---

3. Hart, *Me, Myself, and I*, 103.

the one who died for us and rose again, links us not only to the fellowship of his sufferings, but also to the power of his resurrection. This power is available to us so we can live without being crippled by shame.

In particular, looking to Jesus who loves us unconditionally, opens up a new freedom to relate to others. Shame is a social disgrace. Its power comes from being *seen* negatively, including of our self by our self. So relief comes from being *seen* positively. It begins with God seeing us and extending grace, but it can be wonderfully reinforced by others who also see us but do not condemn us. We are fortunate if we have around us people who know how to extend empathy and acceptance and can put that into words that our damaged heart can hear.

Our new shame-free way of relating may indeed firstly be found among friends. Then with their encouragement, it can extend to new relationships in the wider world. But healing of family shame can take much longer. Family ties reach back further into our younger years, and the pain is deeper. Early family rejections and misunderstandings go right to the core of our being and a new sense of belonging and acceptance may take many years to be realised.

Healing can also be found in the valuable pastoral care that an authentic church community can offer to those who are learning to relate in Christ. But when shame is more acute, arising from trauma in childhood, recovery may need to be also mediated through counselling. The woman I mentioned previously who had experienced incest as a child, found healing in Jesus, but it was facilitated by skilled counselling and sustained prayer ministry. Discovering Jesus and restoration through his shameful death and glorious rising does not negate such assistance. Christians who prayerfully offer help through their God-given gifting and training are God's hands of healing.

RISING OUT OF SHAME

When the women in my church found relief through identification with me, it was identification with the shame, but also with the *rising* out of the shame (though this is but a pale picture of the relief available in Jesus).

For an understanding of the power of *rising*, I have been going back to the Apostle Paul's discussion in 1 Corinthians of his experience of shame. For the status-conscious Greek world of the time, it was shameful to be weak; it was shameful to be a slave; it was shameful to be a woman. Above all, it was shameful to identify with a man who had died on a cross at the hands of Roman rulers. Yet Paul, the educated Pharisee who was also a privileged

Roman citizen, allowed himself to be considered "the scum of the earth" for the sake of Christ because he also identified with Jesus' rising.

Once to escape capture and possible death, he was let down over a wall in an undignified basket. At other times he faced trumped-up charges that saw him flogged and in prison. He was ordered to abandon his life's work and forbidden to speak about the crucified Christ. But he welcomed foolishness, weakness, and dishonor, embracing the shame as an opportunity for the power of God to be seen in his life because his identification was not only with his Master's death, but also with his rising. His position of weakness provided the opportunity for the strength of God to be seen in him.

So Paul urges his readers not only to look to the cross but to also identify with Jesus in his resurrection—the supreme symbol of overcoming shame. When we open our self to God's acceptance and grace, the *rising* does so much more than remove shame. It brings a new Holy Spirit-given way to flourish—living fully with confidence and courage.

THE LIE ABOUT BEING A WOMAN

Nevertheless, in the here and now we are never totally free from the possibility of shame, even when we have found great relief through Jesus' cross and resurrection. Every time we seek to be vulnerable enough to enter into a relationship with another person, we can again feel exposed and sometimes that causes us to retreat from life-giving connection. There are, however, some useful practices of resistance we can embrace so that shame does not make us retreat from all that God calls us to. Brené Brown suggests several: recognise your shame and what triggers it; name it to take away its power; reach out to an empathetic person who will understand and encourage you; and in particular, be aware of what the lie is telling you about yourself.[4]

It is the lie about the shame and the limitations of being a woman that we address here. This lie makes our life uncomfortable, makes us want to hide. It disrupts our relationships and isolates us from both loved ones and new connections. It also limits our service to others. Who am I, we say, to offer help to others? They may push me away if they know how soiled or unreliable or frightened I am inside! How could God possibly welcome someone like me into gospel service?

---

4. Brown, *Daring Greatly,* 74–75.

IS IT FINISHED?

The pastor in one church I knew had a practice when he conducted the communion service of holding up the glass representing Christ's shed blood and declaring, "It is finished!" He was quoting the words that rang out from Jesus as he hung on the cross, surrendering his life. For Jesus it was a cry of triumph—his work of dying and rising again was about to be completed. The great reversal of God's spoilt creation began as new life in Christ became possible.

I knew in my head this glorious gospel promise was available to all—men and women and I could rejoice in what the Scriptures state so clearly. But in my heart, I felt that it was not always applied to women. Full acceptance was not evident. So was Christ's restoring work not finished? Did the great reversal not do it for women? Apparently, there was still something wrong with us that the cross could not fix. I had experienced it in society, in my studies, in my professional work, even in the church.

There is a rebuttal in the gospel records to this implied deficiency in Christ's redeeming work—a little detail I love in the descriptions of Jesus' death as told by Matthew and Mark. When Jesus had breathed his last, they report, "At that moment the curtain of the temple was torn in two from top to bottom" (Matt 27:51; Mark 15:38). It is a dramatic picture of the access to the holy God that became available to everyone because of Jesus' death. It is especially poignant for women and foreigners, because the Jerusalem temple of Jesus' day allowed only Hebrew males to come close to the altar where the priests offered sacrifices. Women and Gentiles were restricted to their outer courts. And only the High Priest, and that only once a year, could enter the most holy part which represented full access to God. It was screened off by a heavy curtain. In a significant divine act, this was the curtain torn open from above at Jesus' death, showing that now all, without distinction, could approach the high and holy God. That *all*, includes women.

There is not something wrong with women that cannot be restored in the new creation. The repair is made effective by Jesus' death and resurrection, though we may only glimpse it now. It will be fully realised when Jesus returns and completes the bringing in of his kingdom.

So we must say it again: there is nothing inherently wrong in being a woman. We are wonderfully and intentionally made by a good Creator who delights in us. God has offered us in Jesus a solution to the shame and guilt that started in the Garden of Eden and gives us the Holy Spirit who goes on perfecting us to become more and more like the unblemished Christ. One day we will delight in unfettered entrance to God's presence with profound joy.

A GOOD LONG LOOK AT JESUS

The lie of our inadequacy as women, of our limitations, of our shame, goes so deep however, I want in concluding this chapter to suggest additional fuel to push back against this falsehood. There is nothing better for appreciating our worth than a good long look at Jesus and his interactions with women in his earthly life. He is the model of how women should be viewed. The limitations that are applied to women in the family, in the church, even in the wider society are certainly not part of Jesus' interactions with them. Dare any of us suggest an attitude that is other than that Jesus displayed!

First-century Palestine is not our world, and so we often do not notice how radical Jesus' actions and words were. In a patriarchal society, Jesus clearly did not treat women as second-class people or dangerous to his purity. He welcomed them into his circle and defied the restrictions his culture and the hyper-religiosity of the Pharisees imposed on them. He raised the eyebrows of those observing him. They were quick to see he was offering women a different way to think about themselves. His enemies even tried to use his known sympathy for women to trap him, expecting him to condemn the woman caught in adultery, though they were not consistent enough to haul the offending man into the stone-throwing circle with her!

STARTING WITH MARY

For examples of Jesus' treatment of specific women, we will start as we did the previous chapter, with Mary. Protestants have long been wary of focusing on Mary the mother of Jesus for fear of making her an object of worship or at least, of excessive veneration. For most of my early life, I do not think I heard a sermon about her outside the Christmas narratives, where the focus is clearly and naturally on the baby. I also think that many preachers have not wanted to hold up a woman as an illustration of courage combined with devotion, though there are Old Testament examples in Ruth, Deborah, and Esther. But the daring commitment of this young girl in saying yes to God is worthy of great admiration and a model for women. I have sought to capture some of that in the epilogue to this book.

Mary did not always understand what her son was doing and saying, but she was there at the cross, a silent witness sharing the gruesome spectacle of her son dying in the most shameful and painful way Roman military-might could devise. In his book discussing the Apostle Paul's 1 Corinthians 13 essay on love, Kenneth Bailey cites Mary as a poignant example of enduring, persevering love[5] and that love was honored by Jesus in his care for her in those last moments of his earthly life. We read later in the Book of Acts that she was in the upper room praying with the other loyal followers after Jesus' ascension and she was possibly there with them when the Holy Spirit fell at Pentecost.

THE OTHER MARYS

Then there are the other Marys. As we saw in Luke 8, at least one Mary was among the women who travelled from Galilee with Jesus. Most of these female disciples were drawn from families of fishermen or subsistence farmers in the north of Palestine, but others such as Joanna and Susanna came from households with more resources and were an essential part of his support team. As unusual as this was, it apparently gave no cause for scandal and illustrates how comfortable they and Jesus' other disciples were in this mixed company, taking their cue from Jesus' own attitude.

At least two Marys were with the women planning to anoint Jesus' body after his death (Mark 16:1–8; Luke 23:55—24:10). It was these women who were entrusted with the earth-shattering good news of Jesus' resurrection and were the first to share this discovery with the other disciples. In his gospel, John singles out Mary Magdalene as the first to encounter the risen Christ and give witness to his living reality. This was a significant choice in a society where a women's testimony was not acceptable in a court of law.

Earlier in his travels, Jesus had already shown unusual acceptance of women—of the "sinful" one caught in adultery; the hemorrhaging "unclean" woman healed of a 12-year flow of blood who was not supposed to be out in public; the audacious Gentile woman pleading with him to heal her child; the woman, or maybe two women, who at different times let down their hair in public to anoint and wipe his feet. This was greatly countercultural.

In the notable episode at Jacob's well in Samaria, we can see this played out in the surprise of Jesus' disciples coming back from fetching lunch and finding him speaking at length to a disreputable woman. In his friendship with Mary and Martha, unmarried women living with their brother in Bethany, Jesus again challenged the contemporary view of women in a patriarchal society whose religious leaders modelled a very low view of women and ascribed to the Talmud teaching not to speak "excessively" with a woman lest this lead them astray. At different times he engaged Martha in

---

5. 1 Corinthians 13:7. The whole verse reads: [Love] "always protects, always trusts, always hopes, always endures." Bailey, *Paul through Mediterranean Eyes*, Loc. 4347, Kindle.

robust theological debate and in one interaction he specifically commended Mary for wanting to learn at the feet of the Master, despite the ethos of the time saying women should not be exposed at all to the holy Scriptures or be expected to learn in the same way men did.

WOMEN IN JESUS' TEACHING

Jesus used a woman to represent God in the parable of the lost coin and in his gospel, Luke often pairs the portrayals of women with corresponding men in a way that shows the worth of the women in a truly ground-breaking way. Examples include Mary's positive acceptance of the angel's message to her, contrasted with the skeptical response of Zacharias, father-to-be of John the Baptist, to the angel; the "sinner" woman who anoints Jesus' feet and seen by Simon the Pharisee after he had neglected the common courtesy in his home of washing his guest's feet; the bent woman healed in the synagogue compared favorably with the condemning synagogue ruler; and the poor widow giving her all in the temple showing up the rich men there.[6] These incidents illustrate the revolutionary truth of the new era Jesus introduces, foreseen by Mary his mother in her Magnificat:

> "He has brought down rulers from their thrones
> but has lifted up the humble" (Luke 1:52).

Given the attitude of the founder of the Christian faith, it is not surprising that the Book of Acts records the early church having women such as Phoebe, Priscilla, Lydia, Junia, and Philip's prophesying daughters among its leaders and teachers.[7] They contribute to the rapid spread of Christianity as, under the impetus of the Holy Spirit, the church moves its focus from the apostles' leadership in Jerusalem to Syrian Antioch and the rest of the Roman world, especially through the house churches.

Dorothy Sayers sums up this picture we get of Jesus in the gospels. Hers are well-known words but worth quoting again:

> Perhaps it is no wonder that the women were first at the Cradle and last at the Cross. They had never known a man like this Man—there never has been such another. A prophet and teacher who never nagged at them, never flattered or coaxed or patronized; who never made arch jokes about them, never treated them either as "The women, God help us!" or "The ladies, God bless them!"; who rebuked without querulousness and praised

---

6. Luke 1; 7:36–50; 13:10–17; 21:1–4.
7. Hill, *Holding up Half the Sky*, details the New Testament examples in his chapter 2.

without condescension; who took their questions and arguments seriously; who never mapped out their sphere for them, never urged them to be feminine or jeered at them for being female; who had no axe to grind and no uneasy male dignity to defend; who took them as he found them and was completely unself-conscious. There is no act, no sermon, no parable in the whole Gospel that borrows its pungency from female perversity; nobody could possibly guess from the words and deeds of Jesus that there was anything "funny" about woman's nature.[8]

THE DANCE BEYOND SHAME

There is a Greek word, *perichoresis,* used down the centuries to describe oneness within the Godhead of Father, Son and Holy Spirit. It is the name of a circle dance—a dance of equals, giving and receiving, each in perfect unison. It has also the idea of indwelling, of oneness, because the participants in this Godhead dance are not separate entities, but one God.[9]

Perichoresis is also a good way to picture our new status as redeemed women. We are invited into the God relationship, not because we have ceased to be separate individuals, but because we are able, without shame, to enjoy the divine friendship. Accepted by God, accepting our self, accepting others who are different from us, we participate in the flow of God and join a dance of abandon with our Creator. This can indeed be vibrant new life without shame.[10]

Personal Reflection

Whose approval matters most to you?

Can you recount a time when shame hindered a relationship that was important to you?

When Jesus invites you to dance will you respond and join in because you trust him (even if you think you are a poor dancer)?

Lewis Smedes describes *shame* as heavy, and *grace* as light. He makes a list for himself to celebrate the lightness grace brings. He begins with,

---

8. Sayers, *Are Women Human?*, 68–69.

9. More recently commentators such as Jurgen Moltmann, Miroslav Volf and Richard Rohr have found the circle dance a useful way to explore the theology of the Trinity.

10. Some material in this chapter first appeared in Turner, "Naked in Eden." and in Turner, "Shame!"

- I believe that the only self I need to measure up to is the self my Maker meant me to be.
- I believe that I am accepted by the grace of God without regard to my deserving.[11]

What statements of faith would you add to Smedes' list to express the lightness of grace that Jesus has brought you?

---

11. Smedes, *Shame and Grace*, 167.

9

Invitations for this Season of your Life

Aged Yet Most Colourful
I am like the autumn leaf in
the latter part of life's circle,
aged yet most colourful.
God is like the earth and the trunk that provide
ongoing nurture for survival
to move through the predetermined cycle of
life;
budding,
blossoming,
and deepening in colour,
until separation.

—Helen Maiden (1935–2017)

THE SEASONS OF LIFE

Our life may take us from place to place, or country to country, but our travels are not only across land or sea borders. Growth to maturity and wisdom and effectiveness means that we are always being prompted out of settled security to journey through the seasons of human existence—birth to childhood, on to adolescence, to young adulthood, through middle age and the season of maturity, hoping to reach retirement, but somewhat wary of what follows in old age and death. No sooner have we mastered (or given up on) the tasks of one stage than the next one looms. It is always unchartered territory for us because we have never been there before.

New territory can be daunting. Whenever God's people in the Bible stories had to move on, they encouraged one another by remembering how God had been with them in the past. We see this supremely in Stephen's sermon in Acts 7. He recounts how God appeared to Abraham in ancient Mesopotamia; was with Joseph in alien Egypt; called Moses in the desert of Midian; then travelled with the Israelites through the wilderness in a movable tent to the promised land. Wherever the people went, God was with them. For Stephen this was a metaphor for God leading these people into a new Jesus-focused era, but it must have also been a great encouragement to Stephen himself as he faced his ultimate test, a martyr's death. It is encouragement for us today too, because as we traverse life's seasons, they need not frighten us or be barriers to fulfilling God's purpose for us, because we too do not walk alone. As Helen Maiden says in her poem, the seasons are God's "predetermined cycle of life." Their demands and opportunities are a normal part of human existence, just as are the ordinary daily tasks of washing and cooking, eating, earning a living, raising children, and mowing the lawn.

THE INVITATIONS OF EACH STAGE

Bruce Turley likens the human journey to a stream whose water flows relentlessly to its destination.[1] You cannot stop the stream running downhill under gravity, but sometimes something blocks its way, and the captured water is diverted to a lagoon and becomes stagnant. It needs to be released to again flow downhill because that is its nature and that is what keeps it fresh. Similarly, as we move inevitably into each season of our life as the years roll on, we find each bend of the river, each turning point, has its own built-in challenges and opportunities. We flow on or stagnate according to how we react to them. Our spiritual and emotional development depends on recognising and responding to what Turley calls the *invitations* of each stage of life.

Invitation suggests more than just undertaking the tasks of that stage. *Invitation* implies openings to be grasped and enjoyed and learnt from,

---

1. Turley, *Turning Points*, 62.

perhaps opportunities to serve and grow. Women on the way to finding their voice need to recognise the *invitations* of each season and see them as part of the process of uncovering who they are and what God's trajectory is asking of them.

However, if your life has been anything but normal, with trauma or early loss of significant family members, for example, the life tasks of grieving and recovery may add an extra dimension to the journey towards all you are meant to be. Most of us experience these stage changes as both consolation and desolation, good and bad, challenge and opportunity to grow, but if yours has been a particularly bumpy journey, be kind and patient with yourself, knowing the God who loves you will walk with you.

BEGINNING WITH BIRTH

Madeleine L'Engle has penned a wonderfully evocative description of the trauma of childbirth. In her poetic imagining, she sees Rachel, beloved wife to the patriarch Jacob, giving birth to Joseph. For him, as for all of us, birth means the death of the familiar and comfortable womb, as he is pushed out into the harsh light of day. We know the end of the story, that Joseph survived, but who knew then that his life would include slavery in Egypt and ruling in Egypt, rejection by his brothers and saving his father and brothers? It all lay before him in this tumultuous beginning. None of it would have been his if he had stayed in the comfort of the womb.

We personally, of course, have no conscious agency in our own birth event, but birth itself is a paradigm of the drama and uncertainty of the seasons of life, especially of the transition from one season to another. Without birth there is no life, and without struggle and new learnings, there is no movement towards the next horizon. But getting to that new place is often dramatic and difficult.

For women making adult life transitions, some stages are more difficult than others. I am addressing those in which women may be tempted to divert or stagnate midstream:

> Entering adulthood
> > Letting go of children
> > > Taking responsibility for aging parents
> > > > Menopause
> > > > > Major change of direction in work or ministry life
> > > > > > Retirement.

ENTERING ADULTHOOD

In our contemporary western world, life events marking entry into adulthood usually include getting a driver's license, higher education or further training, a first job, and leaving home. Even though these may be relatively small challenges, they are significant ones, leading to the bigger steps of career, partnering and children. Women emerge into adult life at different times and probably there is more variation between women than for men. For me, finishing my study (so I thought), moving to America, marrying, and entering my first professional position as a town planner, happened all at once at the age of twenty-three. I have a sister-in-law who married at eighteen—her higher education and childbearing came much later. Other women are mothers by the age of twenty. Some are never mothers—by choice or biology. So there is no specific age for entering adult life, but it is characterised by consciously making life decisions for oneself and not just going with the family or the culture's flow. We can think of it as putting a toe in the wider world.

I suspect that for women younger than me there is a greater awareness that you do not have to automatically follow a pattern handed down to you. Women of my era simply assumed that when we were about twenty-five, we would marry and have children, combining that is some way with a career and the aspirations of our husband. We knew we had many more opportunities than our mothers, especially in education, but often we could not see clear markers in an unmapped landscape. I knew I had a strong call to serve God, perhaps as a missionary overseas, but expected it would be within the other taken-for-granted parameters of my life, such as marriage and children and my husband's agricultural research. I accepted these as givens.

I admire the seriousness and independence with which younger women are contemplating their futures today, not just drifting with external expectations laid on them. My three daughters-in-law (to whom this book is dedicated) are part of Gen X. Western society has told them "they can have it all" but like many of their generation, they have discovered the reality is they cannot if they want children. They have however made the choices and embraced the necessary compromises to enter fully into adult life.

In my second round of tertiary study, I remember one day juggling its demands with the needs of a sick child. Feeling sorry for myself, I reflected on Jesus speaking of the choices that following him entailed. He put it rather starkly. There were eunuchs who were born that way, he said, and there were those who chose to live like eunuchs for the sake of the kingdom of heaven (Matt 19:12). Yes, I realised, there are some things I have to forgo for the sake of God's kingdom. It does not seem fair, but perhaps this is what it means to consent to being a eunuch! Not having it all!

I did, as it happens, continue my study, and in retrospect should have engaged my husband more intentionally in the family tasks of that stage of life, but at least I was making conscious choices about what was most important. Later, when grandchildren were appearing on the scene, there were other choices to be made. How available would I be for child-care, when God's direction was pointing to increasing opportunities to teach overseas?

Making choices and choosing timing are the essential tasks of the opening-up stage in which much is still possible, even if not all at once. Self-awareness and a keen ear to hear God's wisdom, are the essential tools for navigating these years and continuing to find your voice.

Like birth, early adulthood can be a time of turbulence, of consciously choosing a new way to live or to enter into new, deeper relationships. I have used the expression *leaving home* in chapter 4 to describe entering the larger stage of life which must be chosen and passed through to finding your voice. The move out of your physical home can be done overnight (with some help with the boxes) and may signal the first taking responsibility for yourself. However, leaving home psychologically and emotionally may be spread out over a decade or so. Or only completed later. Some women find that it only really happens in midlife when the pressured years of child-raising are easing off.

MIDLIFE

At some points in your life, the turning points will be obvious and crucial, and you will see more clearly that even crises offer creative possibilities for growth and new direction. For women in particular, midlife can be particularly stretching, yet filled with open invitations.

Three major tasks of midlife are here in focus—letting go of your children, taking on responsibility for aging parents, and menopause. Those who find themselves in this season are called the sandwich generation for a reason. These three challenges are normal and expected experiences that impact everyone in some form. The difficulty is that sometimes all three arrive together. For a woman seeking to find her voice, these are passages to be negotiated before emerging into the wide-open spaces of the next phase of life's journey.

LETTING GO OF YOUR CHILDREN[2]

How difficult it is to practice what you preach. For a number of years, I was aware that one of the challenges of parenting in midlife was the gracious letting go of your children. When my husband and I reached this season, we found the going a bit rough and our emotions rather raw. First there was the leaving behind of two university sons when we moved out of the city to be closer to the church I pastored. It did not help to remind myself that my parents did the same thing—leaving behind all three of their newly-adult children in one part of the country when they moved to another part for similar reasons. Then our eldest son married, and we "lost" him to another woman and another family. And then the second, and then the third, the baby who stayed longest, were gone.

We were always pleased about these developments, of course. We were proud of our children making their way in the world, just as my parents were proud of their children and the choices my brothers and I made. I remember with regret, however, that in my teenage rows with my mother, I discovered that the best way to hurt her was to remind her it was her job to make me independent of her. She should not keep trying to tell me how to live! I knew it all (so I thought)! Independence was the goal!

Generation after generation has had to make these transitions. But in the fast-changing western world the territory is even less charted than it used to be. There are fewer rites of passage. Families, particularly blended ones, are more complicated in their structure and expectations, and longer education or unemployment postpone the time of leaving. Profiles of Millennials refer to developmental delay, a reluctance to take responsibility, and with the phenomenon of "boomerang" children, especially in unstable periods such as the Covid-19 pandemic, there may be more than one time of leaving. As a consequence, the final break may not be recognised until after it has occurred—neither celebrated nor mourned. So when does the mid-life parent actually "let go"?

For women in the workplace, continuing responsibility for their children is the tension that complicates aspirations for a wider role in career or society. The way of life that became a guilt-filled juggling act with school-age children, may continue even when they are grown, because the juggling now involves expectations about care for grandchildren. I know women who have surrendered significant opportunities because grandchildren appeared on the scene and the parents expected her to be continuously available. That is not always the best solution for either the parents or the children and it

---

2. Some of this chapter first appeared in Turner, "Letting Go . . ."

may also be too early for the grandmother to disconnect from the wider world.

Grandchildren are an unsurpassed delight for most of us. Neither I nor our sons had much contact with our grandparents because we lived far from each other, so I was determined it would be different for the next generation. With my eight grandchildren, their primary school years in particular have been a rich time of connecting and caring. I have valued the interactions with them, but not to the exclusion of all else.

For women whose identity has been tied exclusively to parenting, letting go of children (and grandchildren) may be particularly hard. It produces a major reassessment of who they are and how they relate to the world. I recall the woman who came to work with my planning firm in the United States because she was in danger of drowning in a sea of lost identity. A mother before she was twenty, at the early age of forty her children had flown the nest, yet her whole adult life had centred on mothering. Still now only in early midlife, she felt she had lost the one thing she was supposed to be doing, and that well before the time when physical reproduction had ceased—a cultural rather than a biological menopause.

Godly balance requires us to encourage our adult children to take responsibility for their lives but continue to value their relationships within the wider family and stay connected. This is the equivalent in this stage of life of the Apostle Paul's even-handed approach to the tug of war between the generations: "Children, obey your parents in everything, for this pleases the Lord. Fathers, do not embitter your children, or they will become discouraged" (Col 3:20–21). How can we let go in a way that helps them observe the commandment? Our continuing to give orders, or worse, manipulating them into meeting our wishes, is not helpful either. We should let go in a way that makes it easier for them to give due weight to the shape of both their family and their community.

Boomerang adult children, who return once or more to the nest, present an additional challenge. In the time they were independent they had considerable freedom to do as they wished. Now back in the family home for whatever reason, they may resent losing that freedom, yet the parents are right to expect some family protocols be discussed and followed.

When I had trouble letting go, I tried to examine what was driving me. Was I wanting to protect my children from the mistakes I had made or the evils I had seen? Maybe, just maybe, I was trying to live through them, asking from them what the structure of family relationships was never meant to provide. The truth of the matter is that we do not need to let go of our children—not totally. How can a mother forget the child she bore? We are bound together in a structure of mutual responsibility which never ceases.

What we need to let go of is our control, our agenda, and give our children the freedom of responsibility under God, as indeed, God does with us. That gives us new freedom too.

A better understanding of the role of the parent in fostering independence would be to see it as a transfer process—encouraging the child to gradually move their dependency on their parents to depending on God. The young adult is taking responsibility, but with careful understanding of the Master's instructions and relying on the Holy Spirit's help. This is the answer to both excessive independence and excessive dependence and the idea behind the "meek shall inherit the earth." A meek horse is one broken in so that it obeys, but whose whole spirit and energy is available to fulfil all the horse was created to be. Within the family structure of respect and loyalty and responsibility, our "meek" children can move towards their full potential.

TAKING RESPONSIBILITY FOR AGING PARENTS

Sometimes there is no distance between the letting go of our children and taking on responsibility for our parents. There is only one biblical commandment addressed to family relationships: "Honor your father and mother." What are the implications of this for the midlife woman (because it is the woman who usually bears the biggest load of this later form of juggling)? To what degree should this impact on her as she seeks to find her voice?

In seeking to *honor* our parents, many dilemmas present themselves and overturn what we knew in earlier years—that honoring means obeying. How do you care for these increasingly frail people whom you love? What role does independence play for them? At what point should you step in and make decisions about where and how they live?

Take the garden and the house for instance. Some older folks would prefer to stay in their own home as long as possible, no matter how much the garden is getting on top of them and repairs on the house are lapsing. We worry that our parents are expending scarce energy on them and hastening their death. Be sensible, we want to tell them. Or perhaps we do not want to see them fritter away their resources unnecessarily or leave a massive clean-up operation for us at the end. Whose interests are served by the decisions we make on behalf of our parents? What does it mean to *honor* them in these complex choices?

For my husband and me, our habit of making decisions and acting quickly on them, meant that we downsized our house and garden with only a short interval between informing our family and acting on it. That we did not consult them points to a desire for total independence we may later regret when we need their help. The biblical command to honor your parents acknowledges the structure of inter-dependence required to live as people made in the image of the relationship God. We were not created to be totally autonomous. I know that sometimes by valuing independence we mean taking responsibility for oneself—not sponging off nor blaming another for one's own life. But God did not intend that we live without giving and taking in a mutually supportive way.

So *honor* in the fifth commandment addresses family relationships that continue to matter, even though the actual details and responsibilities may alter at different stages of life and in changing cultural patterns. Lewis Smedes renders *honor* as "give due weight to"—a moral choice to observe the shape of the relationships with loyalty and respect, no matter the cost. This acknowledges a calling from God to fulfil our role in the grand design. The "commandment with a promise" (Eph 6:2) suggests that when family relationships are structured this way, we will reap a benefit equivalent to that offered to the agrarian people of the Old Testament—"living long in the land"—security and contentment.

The example of course, is Jesus. He submitted to his parent's authority when he was young, but gradually his life's mission took precedence, at times even seeming to conflict with family ties. Yet at the cross, his "behold your mother" to disciple John was a handing over of care for her, acknowledging a continuing love and responsibility.

MENOPAUSE

The third task of midlife for women is what we loosely call menopause. By menopause, we are usually referring here to the whole season of a woman's "change of life," starting with perimenopause. This includes the actual last menstrual cycle, and maybe a year or two after it—anything between the two and ten years that the woman's body takes to prepare for and adjust to the cessation of menstruation. There is an emerging literature giving advice to women to listen to the invitations of this season and embrace them.[3]

I remember when I was fifteen visiting with my mother at the home of two of her aunts who lived in a tiny hamlet on the edge of the National Park near Sydney. While my brothers played on the beach, I was within earshot of the women as they chatted. Suddenly they dropped their voices, and I could no longer hear what they were saying. Then came my mother's words, "Well,

---

3. Readers familiar with Gail Sheehy's *Passages: Predictable Crises of Adult Life* may be interested to note she also wrote *Menopause: The Silent Passage* (1991).

she is a girl. She has to know about this sometime." They were discussing menopause, but it was at that time and for many years after, a taboo topic in polite company and many of us were ignorant about it until it arrived.

Fortunately, my family did not pass on any of the dire warnings that some daughters receive about "the change," but I joined with other women as we recounted to each other the woes of hot flushes and sleepless nights. In contrast, several writers now urge women to take the opportunity menopause brings to understand their body better, to look forward to an expansive future and frame positively what is happening to them in this very normal season of life. Cheryl Bridges Johns, for example, calls perimenopause a "kairos" moment—God's time of opportunity—and suggests seven transforming gifts of menopause that can be grasped in a spiritual journey which starts with debunking the negative myths.[4] She urges us to go with courage into the next phase of life and service in much the same way as this book does, but through the lens of introspection that menopause can give rise to.

In her *Theology of the Womb*, Christy Angelle Bauman casts a wider net, discussing the many seasons of a woman's body and viewing God through the symbolism of blood. Her chapter on menopause again puts as much emphasis on the gains as on its losses.

Many have been helped by Richard Rohr's description of the spiritual challenges and opportunities of the second half of life in his *Falling Upward* and it is in this spirit that menopause is important for women journeying to find their voice. Rather than seeing life closing down, or as an excuse to feel sorry for yourself as a woman, a positive attitude to this change (and shared information and support) can open up life in a wonderful way as you respond to the invitations of this season. Even as you read this, if you are nowhere near approaching your fifties, store in the back of your mind that all is not over when you hit the mid-century. Menopause comes with new promises as well as new assessments of who you are in the hands of your Creator. And a few less things to give attention to!

RETIREMENT OR A MAJOR CHANGE OF DIRECTION?

Some years ago, my husband and I visited Jordan on our way to Israel. Jordan is best known to tourists as the home of Petra—the magnificently preserved

---

4. Johns, *Seven Transforming Gifts* lists these transforming gifts as uncovering, anger, authentic self, expanded time, spiritual freedom, vision, and courage.

city, hidden to sight through a narrow rock defile until you are almost upon it. It is probably on the bucket list of everyone venturing to the Middle East.

Of course, we went to Petra first, but it is Jordan's Mt Nebo that stays in my mind. This was where Moses, at the end of forty years of shepherding Israelite stragglers across the desert, climbed the mountain and finally glimpsed the destination. Moses himself was not to cross the Jordan River into the Promised Land so it was the (incomplete) end of the road for him.

We too climbed Mt Nebo and there I cried for Moses. He was a courageous leader, holding in faith for so long God's promise to Israel of a secure homeland. That he would glimpse, but not possess the promise, was just cruel in my eyes. No doubt I was identifying with Moses, not for any parallel of leading a multitude, but as the holder of a vision in which I saw my own involvement coming to a conclusion.

Having a goal, being prepared to challenge the status quo for the sake of that vision, has always defined me. I look for it also in all whom I mentor. Where are you heading? Who has God made you to be? What is your unique mix of creation gifts and Spirit-given gifts? Claim the faith of the Hebrews 11 heroes and trust God! Launch out! Dare to be a Daniel! Lead the people, Deborah! Get out of the boat, Peter!

I say it to you too, through this book. It has always been my passion for the women around me. Not necessarily to be like me, becoming a pastor in midlife or to breaking new ground in society or in the church, but to know the joy and satisfaction of responding to the God who created you for a purpose and goes on equipping you through the Holy Spirit to bring love and joy to others through your gifts.

But on Mt Nebo, I was grieving for what personally I had *not* achieved, where I had fallen short of my long-held goals. Perhaps those goals had been unrealistic, but I was very aware that by my society's expectations, I was approaching my use-by date. What was there left for me to aim at? Would I ever have a vision or goals again? Was retirement next? That felt deadly.

THE RELATIONSHIP IS WHAT MATTERS

Something Ruth Haley Barton has written finally helped me at this stage of life. She imagines Moses on Mt Nebo at peace, not regretful, as God gives him the glimpse over the Jordan. Though he is tantalizingly close to the Promised Land, what he looks forward to is even better. He anticipates his final union with God—the God who called him and has been with him the whole of the journey. "Finally there would be nothing standing between him and the lover of his soul . . . *for Moses the presence of God was the Promised*

Land. Next to that, everything else had already paled in significance."[5] The psalmist, long after Moses, will put this hope into words, "As for me, I will be vindicated and will see your face; when I awake, I will be satisfied with seeing your likeness" (Ps 17:15).

More significant visionaries than I have pondered the ambivalence of the view from Mt Nebo. In Martin Luther King Jr.'s last speech in Memphis the night before his assassination his words rang out:

> Like anybody, I would like to live a long life. Longevity has its place. But I am not concerned about that now. I just want to do God's will. And He's allowed me to go up to the mountain. And I've looked over, and I've seen the promised land.
>
> I may not get there with you, but I want you to know tonight that we as a people will get to the promised land.
>
> So I'm happy tonight. I'm not worried about anything. I'm not fearing any man. "Mine eyes have seen the glory of the coming of the Lord."[6]

For Martin Luther King, it did not fully work out how he hoped, though his life and martyrdom had a profound and honored legacy. That there is a Black Lives Matter movement fifty years later shows there is still much to be realised of his vision.

For myself, out of the sadness I felt on Mt Nebo, came a search for what God had for me in the next season. It was teaching in Africa and Asia. This made sense when I looked at my life experience: extensive travels had given me competence and ease in living cross-culturally; I had good links to both Africa and Asia through my husband's research; and I had lived previously on both continents. It took a while, however, for me to find what shape that work would take.

A newspaper article at the time highlighting the plight of women in developing countries coincided with my meeting a man from Dallas who with his wife and several African colleagues, had begun a ministry training pastors in the back-blocks of east African countries. In these isolated areas where Christians have few resources and even less money for training, a new model was envisioned to provide materials and week-long conferences for pastors and church leaders—women as well as men—who had no other access to Bible resources. My ministry over these past ten years was born out of those tears on Mt Nebo. It has given me wonderful friends and colleagues in many places and a sense of *rightness* for this season of my life. I truly feel, as in the poem above, like a colorful autumn leaf in the latter part of life's cycle.

5. Barton, *Strengthening the Soul*, 214.
6. Quoted by Yancey in *Soul Survivor*, 39–40.

RETIREMENT

Some years ago, there was a bumper sticker that read, *Get even with your children—Live long enough to be a burden to them!* My sons always had a light-hearted answer to that: *Treat us right* or *we'll put you in a home!* We were not so far away from retirement then that the implied reversal of power and responsibility, had a slight sting in its jest.

When my husband and I relinquished our fulltime paid jobs, we thought of it at first as retirement. That was part of my anguish on Mt Nebo. It felt like life was just about over! I found it hard to let go of my role in the final congregation I pastored. In our family, I resisted handing on social responsibilities to my sons and daughters-in-law. No longer hosting Christmas dinner, for example, was surprisingly difficult, even though we had moved to a smaller house where whole family activities were not easy to accommodate. However, a wonderful new ministry has opened for me, while my husband continues his science work with students in many countries, but at a lesser pace. We truly appreciate still having satisfying and useful activities and receive them as God's grace to us.

A friend who is ninety years old and a much-valued spiritual director of many people over the years, recently told me he had just heard God tell him to retire! I explored what that meant for him, not believing he could ever retire. For health reasons, he needs to cut back on his commitments, he said, with fewer appointments and less structure in his day. That may be sensible, but I know that anytime someone sits down with him in conversation, he will continue to give them his gifts of insight, spiritual direction, and unconventionality. His ministry continues.

John Piper has written a little book called *Rethinking Retirement.* He urges us to resolutely resist the kind of retirement that is self-indulgent consumerism, with no awareness of the world's deep needs. He reminds us that our life's purpose—to bring glory to Christ—still applies. But to those who are afraid of disappointing God or themselves by their diminishing energy, he passes on Charles Spurgeon's wisdom in the reassurance that God kisses away the fear of aging with abundant promises of his continuing presence.

Awareness of others, and of our self and our gifting, is just as important in the last stage of life as it was earlier. There is no shortage of opportunities to bless others. The world is hungry for gentle service and wisdom, given with grace. The Apostle Paul's assurance that "he who began a good work in you will carry it on to completion until the day of Christ Jesus" (Phil 1:6) is an anthem for retirement too!

A WAY TO THINK OF LIFE'S SEASONS—DESOLATION AND CONSOLATION

One of my sons once asked if I would like to be twenty again. No, I said, I would like the energy again, but not give up the wisdom gained over the years. That would be too high a cost.

The world is full of rhythms. Sunrise and sunset. Summer and winter. Seedtime and harvest. Something gone and something gained. There are losses to mourn and invitations to embrace. High energy periods but wisdom not yet won. Children to hug and children to let go. Experiences to revel in, and later to pass on, sharing what we have created and watching others tread the path we have blazed.

Like childbirth, new life comes out of pain. In the desolation, we experience God's apparent absence and welcome his return with joy. Let me encourage you to recognize where you are in these cycles because that will give you the agenda for ongoing living. Accepting the invitations of each season from among multiple choices offered, simplifies the call to follow without fear where God is leading. God's words through Isaiah to the people of Israel apply in all the seasons of life:

> Listen to me, you descendants of Jacob,
>   all the remnant of the people of Israel,
> you whom I have upheld since your birth,
>   and have carried since you were born.
> Even to your old age and gray hairs
>   I am he, I am he who will sustain you.
> I have made you and I will carry you;
>   I will sustain you and I will rescue you (Isa 46:3–4).

Personal Reflection

"We neither make nor save ourselves. God does both the making and saving. He creates each of us by Christ Jesus to join him in the work he does, the good work he has gotten ready for us to do, work we had better be doing" (Eph 2:9–10 The Message).

As you identify the season you are in, can you see how you are changing and growing through it? Ask yourself,

What is unique about this part of my journey?

What are the invitations to be creative at this time of life?

How can I best grow in my relationship with God and in serving others in this season?

10

The Courage of Faith

Hope is hearing the melody of the future. Faith is to dance to it.
—Rubem Alves (1933–2014)

I BEGAN THIS BOOK encouraging you to tell your story, your many stories, and reflect on your past—who has God made you to be from your creation in the womb, your family environment, and through all your lifetime of experiences, both dramatic and recurring. Where can you see God's footprints early in your life, even when you were not aware of it?

Then the reflection process moved into the present. I suggested you listen to what is happening in your ordinary life, day to day. What themes can you identify as your relationship with God has continued? Understanding these can make you more alert to how God is speaking to you now. How have you been gifted by God? Can you identify roadblocks to responding to God's voice, roadblocks that take shape when you realize what you need to risk in responding to God's call on your life?

By considering the imposter syndrome, for example, you may have identified something in your attitude to yourself or your circumstances that is frightening you or holding you back. Or perhaps your challenge is to care more lovingly for your own body or to move beyond shame by opening your hands to receive God's grace. All this brings you to the current season of your life.

The next step now in finding and using your voice is to look to the future. This is where the courage of faith is needed. This is not blind faith, but faith born of confidence in God, because the opposite of faith is not fear but doubt—doubt that God wants only the best for you, doubt that you are hearing correctly, doubt that your loving Father can carry you through what is asked of you. That is why, as contradictory as it sounds, someone has defined faith as "reason gone courageous." It is eminently reasonable that your Creator will not abandon you after taking such great delight in your creation. It is eminently reasonable that when the Holy Spirit is working in you, remaking you, this project will not be abandoned easily either.

God-believing faith is not passive. It will propel you into adventures you would never have undertaken on your own without a Holy Spirit-given prompting. You might even experience it as a Spirit-given shove! "Now faith is *confidence* in what we hope for and *assurance* about what we do not see," the writer to the Hebrews says (11:1 my emphasis) and goes on to tell us about the heroes of faith who launched out into the deep, trusting God's future for them. God does not expect us to generate in ourselves a kind of blind optimism that says, to use an Australian idiom, "She'll be right, mate!" Or sigh with the more recent expression of resignation, "It is what it is." Nor launch out without counting the cost. Our heavenly Father will give you many and repeated assurances of divine presence with you, but then says, "Get on with it!"

A LIFE GOAL?

Your sense of how to move forward may come from a deep awareness of a life goal which is not yet fulfilled. Our western culture encourages us to have a vision, to reach for the stars, to influence our future. This was the story of Beverley Bass, who in 1986 became the first female captain of an American Airlines commercial plane. From her teenage years she had a passion to fly and worked single-mindedly to find ways to fund her flying lessons, buy a plane, begin her own charter business, and then finally secure a job as a commercial pilot. But beyond that, the challenge remained to be accepted as competent enough to command a plane as its captain. It was a battle against severe odds, some of which still hamper women moving into this role. Even today, she notes, not all passengers realise it is the pilot they are hearing when a female captain welcomes them to the flight over the intercom. For this reason, Beverly initiated an association to encourage women pilots to support each other.

On September 11th, 2001 Captain Bass was flying a Boeing 777 when terrorists attacked the United States. Hers was one of several planes re-directed to land at Gander Airport in Newfoundland, Canada to keep their passengers safe. Her role in this crisis came to public attention when a Broadway musical, *Come from Away*, was written about the arrival of the planes in this isolated area and the welcome the local residents gave them. Later, in 2019, she received the TPG *Hero* Award for leadership for women in commercial aviation, gaining the recognition she deserved. In the interviews that followed she described the singleness of her childhood goal to become a commercial pilot, emphasizing that such goals can only be achieved through great discipline and persistence.

This is an inspiring story, but you may not have had that singleness of vision. And neither did I. However, at a significant point in my life, God gave me a picture that later helped me interpret what was unfolding for me and kept me following God's direction even though I did not comprehend where it was leading.

I can still see in my mind's eye where I was on that day more than forty years ago. I had been sleeping on the sofa in our house in Canberra for a few nights because the birth of our first child was imminent and I was very uncomfortable. For some strange reason, I was pondering the divine rejection of King David's desire to build a house for God to match the splendor of his own newly built royal palace. No, the Lord had said, that will be left to your son Solomon. Your hands are blooded by the battles you have had to fight. Your job is to prepare for the temple, not build it.

At that point in my life, I had no inkling that God would later call me to be a pioneering pastor and I certainly did not know what to make of this picture. As I mentioned previously, my husband and I were strongly committed to encouraging people to serve God in their everyday lives and professions. We had said time and time again: God's work is not limited to ministry in a church; and being a pastor is not the pinnacle of Christian service! Besides, there were no women pastors in my denomination in my part of the world, and no indication that might change. Being a pastor was certainly no goal of mine.

Just as King David was commissioned to bring together the resources, I have subsequently come to see my task has been to open the way for others, especially women, to grow in Christian leadership, including, but not limited to serving as pastors. Only in my last full-time church appointment did I realise senior pastoral leadership myself, and that was the position I relinquished to train pastors, overseas and at home. Clearly, in this second half of my life, my role has been to prepare others. That is truly a privilege, but I needed God's early picture of David paving the way for Solomon to save me from being jealous of the opportunities the women coming behind me would have.

A healing experience at the Californian retreat I mentioned in chapter 1 was another grace that enabled me to go forward with further confidence in this, sure that God was accompanying me. At that retreat, part of my Fuller course with Dallas Willard, we were invited to attend the early morning service conducted every day by the center's residents in the little chapel. As you do, each morning for the week I sat in the same seat. And each morning, just as we came to the part of the service when we said together, "Our Father," the rays of the rising sun came through the window and rested warmly on me. Every morning, I experienced the reassurance I needed that my heavenly Father's care and support was greater than any care my parents could have given me, and more than enough for the journey ahead, whatever that was to be. I felt bathed in the divine parent's love and approval and that was enough. It is enough for you too, even if you cannot identify a life-long goal.

GET OUT OF THE BOAT!

I resonate with the title of John Ortberg's book—*If You Want to Walk on Water, You Have to Get Out of the Boat*. The reference is to Jesus welcoming Peter to join him walking on the stormy water of Lake Galilee (Matt 14:22–33). After the dramatic feeding of the five thousand on the far side of the lake, Jesus had stayed behind for quiet prayer, but in the middle of the night came over the water to the fearful disciples, huddled together in their storm-buffeted boat. In their panic they did not recognise him, thinking it was a ghost. So Jesus' memorable first words to them were, "Take courage! It is I. Don't be afraid."

As the story unfolds, we read that after *walking* on water, Peter *sank* in fear. But he did walk, while the other disciples did not even try. And when he started to sink, Jesus reached out a hand to him and he was safe. Ortberg points out that water-walking in response to God's call is always a matter of choice because we can stay in the boat and be passive observers. However, if despite our fear, we accept the invitation to get out of the boat, we learn to trust, even through our failures. Our courage will grow a little with each venture and each experience of God's power.

Peter's personality may have inclined him more readily than most to dare to do such things, but the gospels and the Book of Acts show us further instances of Jesus calling this impetuous man out of his comfort zone to prepare him for leadership in the early church. Firstly, Peter needed to be tested by the resurrection Master (John 21:15–19) and his faith and love fine-tuned. His is a fascinating story of how God uses even what seems to be a person's weaknesses or peculiarities. Peter's ever-ready mouth blurted out a significant first declaration of Jesus as Messiah, a declaration Jesus commended. But it also led him to make the ridiculous suggestion on the Mount of Transfiguration of preserving the experience by building shelters for the patriarchs and Jesus (Matt 16:16; 17:4). Later he rashly cut off the ear of one of those who came to arrest Jesus. He then went on to betray his Master three times in the high priest's court that night. Again however, it was Peter who was the daring one, in the courtyard near Jesus while most of the other disciples fled, and he was the one who rushed in to see the empty tomb when his companion, John, hesitated at the entrance.

The incident of Peter walking on water is only told by Matthew, and scholars suggest that in selecting the stories for his gospel, Matthew chose those which would most encourage the early church as it confronted persecution. The message of Peter's example is to have courage and trust the Master. I first preached from the walking-on-water story twenty years ago when our church was undertaking a major venture, including building facilities for an innovative spirituality center. We were entering a new era in the life of our congregation, doing something unconventional and taking a risk financially. Money risks bring their own fear! It required faith. Like the disciples, we needed to hear Jesus' words, "Do not be afraid!" and his promise to go with us if we were going to get out of the boat. Faith wrestled with fear, but faith won out and we opened the *Dayspring Centre* later that year.

DO NOT BE AFRAID!

The Scriptures record many occasions when a message from God begins with the words, *"Don't be afraid!"* Communication through an angel carries its own surprise, but even when the call comes by some other means, *"Don't be afraid"* always seems to precede an invitation to undertake a risky action. Zechariah commissioned to be the father of John the Baptist (Luke 1:13) heard it, as did Mary (Luke 1:30) and then Joseph (Matt 1:20). So did the shepherds on the hills outside Bethlehem the night Jesus was born (Luke 2:10). Jesus said it another time to his disciples just before his death (John 14:27) and the angel repeated it to the women at the empty tomb. The Apostle Paul received the instruction in a vision when facing opposition in Corinth (Acts 18:9). And to John on the island of Patmos, Christ says in a dream, *"Do not to be afraid!"* before commissioning him to write down the visions recorded in the book of Revelation.

What all these examples have in common is a call to exercise faith. They also have in common that each person did have courage, despite their fear, to say yes to the commission. Even Zechariah who doubted the angel's words and so was struck dumb for the duration of Elizabeth's pregnancy, did eventually name his son as instructed. Perhaps the invitation to have confidence in God's leading, also helped Zechariah and Elizabeth raise their unusual son for his special role in paving the way for the Messiah. That may not have been an easy task for the elderly parents of a radical young man!

Sheryl Sandberg refers in her book, *Lean in*, to a sign she put up when she was at Facebook to encourage risk-taking and innovation. It said, "What would you do if you weren't afraid?"[1] There is no doubt that many good and necessary things have never been put into action because people were afraid to risk, or stand out from the crowd, or not be liked. But when God says *"Do not be afraid!"* it has a whole greater depth of meaning and promise. The words are not a rebuke for being afraid. Initial fear and awe should be a normal human response to interaction with the divine. To use C. S. Lewis' imagery in the Narnia stories, Jesus is not a tame lion. And an angel coming from the presence of the Lord is not just a neighbourhood buddy. Fear and awe are appropriate reactions.

So if you hear the Master's *"Do not be afraid,"* know that this is probably paving the way for an out-of-the-ordinary call inviting you to participate in God's plan for you. And being God's plan, you are assured of the Holy Spirit's presence and power. Like Peter, your courage to step out of the boat will come from faith in the one who is commissioning you—the courage of *faith in* Jesus. Fear at the enormity of God's commission is not unexpected. The only failing is to not respond with daring and trust in the one who calls you and promises Jesus' presence with you.

RECOGNISING GOD'S VOICE

Before you take the risk to obey, however, you need to be sure it is God's voice you are hearing. Our desires can be very deceiving, our motives mixed. We do not usually hear God in an audible voice, and the message may come through another person or via a dream or vision. But mostly, the call will be in the Holy Spirit's quiet voice, meeting you in your meditation on the Scriptures. Jesus describes his followers as friends, not servants, and friendship implies mutual conversation. The shape of how Jesus wants you to walk and work with him will most likely be worked out in the conversation of everyday life with him.

1. Sandberg, *Lean In*, 25.

If as you have read this book, examined your life experience and gifts, and gained an understanding of where your heart responds with joy to serve those in need, you will recognise the Master's call. In this, Jesus likens us to sheep. Food, safety, and shelter for Palestinian sheep relied on their responding to their shepherd's voice, following him so that at the end of the day he could take them to the safety of home or fold (John 10:3–5).

To learn to recognise Jesus' voice, you must expect that he still speaks today, and that he will speak even to you, however unworthy or small you may feel. You can grow your confidence in this by reminding yourself that it is in the Creator's interests to bring to fruition the gifts planted and grown in you. It is certainly not presumptuous to expect to hear your Shepherd's guiding voice. However, the ability to recognise that voice must be honed by practice in listening and acting on it, starting with the small everyday promptings of the Holy Spirit. We all make mistakes in this, but fortunately, we learn as much from them as from the confirmations that we are hearing God rightly. But on the major decisions, especially regarding details of your call to serve God, ask that it be confirmed specifically from Scripture. Circumstances, or a word from another person who does not know what you are wrestling with, can be additional confirmation. Above all, hearing correctly will require that you are prepared in faith to act on the Master's message.

GOD'S SURPRISING CHOICES

Surprised by what God is asking of you? That has good biblical warrant. God's choices are often startling. Moses and Jeremiah, for example, did not consider they were suitable candidates for what God was requesting of them, but we women can take particular encouragement from the genealogy leading up to the birth of Jesus which begins Matthew's gospel. There are five surprising women mentioned in it, each of them had an unusual background and would not have expected to have such an honored position. In fact, it is even remarkable that their names are there at all, because women were not usually included in a Hebrew genealogy. But there they are, honored forebears of Jesus.

Take Tamar, for example. She had the misfortune to be raped by her half-brother and later presented herself to her father-in-law as a prostitute (Gen 38:1–30) to gain the offspring she was due. Through that very action she has a place in the line of Jesus. In contrast, Rahab, the next mentioned was a professional prostitute, operating from a house on the wall of Jericho, presumably to catch men coming and going through the nearby gate. She believed in the God of Israel, however, and it turned her life around and gave her a heritage in the promised land (Jos 2; 6).

Ruth, a despised Moabitess, showed loyalty to her Israelite mother-in-law and returned with her in poverty to Bethlehem from her foreign birthplace. Through her commitment to God and her mother-in-law, revealing her character through hard and daring work, she was blessed with a considerate husband and a child who was grandfather to King David (Ruth 4:9–17). Three generations later, Bathsheba, wife to Uriah, had no power to repulse that king's attentions and as a result lost her husband and child (2 Sam 11;12). Yet through later marriage to David, she too has her place in the line of Jesus.

Even teenage Mary, the last-named in Matthew's list, though not treated as heinously by others as the first four women, had to endure the potential shame of an out-of-wedlock pregnancy and the challenging first years of motherhood as a refugee, travelling with her young child.

God seems frequently to choose the unexpected in this world. Perhaps that makes it clear that the power and favor come from above. When you answer God's invitation, from whatever season you are in, you may understand your path only sketchily at first, but as it unfolds it will give greater depth and meaning to your life. You will come to relish the opportunities opening to you because you were created for this very purpose. And in the uncertainty and pressure of the challenge, God's presence will be even more real to you as a person of faith.

FAITH IS EXPRESSED IN ACTION

We must note, however, that the kind of faith described in Scripture is one of action—putting your very life on the line. It is more than a warm feeling. James, leader after Peter of the early church, writes in his letter to Christians facing persecution, that faith without deeds is useless (Jas 2:26). He gives the examples of Abraham and Rahab whose trust in God enabled them to take risks and act with courage.

In Hebrews 11, other examples of faith heroes include Noah and his boat. "By faith Noah . . . built an ark to save his family" (Heb 11:7). Someone has described the experience of Noah's family as being shut into a three-story container built in a dry paddock, housing eight people and a menagerie, with no view! And no knowing when it would end. Writing this in a time when many people are experiencing Covid-19 lockdowns of varying kinds and having to shelter for an indefinite period, we can see parallels to Noah and his family's three hundred days of confinement!

I remember an earlier time when this example spoke powerfully to our congregation as we faced a crucial challenge. Our newly established church was developing rapidly, and we had outgrown the small municipal hall where we were meeting. We looked for land to erect an appropriate building, but soon faced sustained and vocal opposition which spilled over into the local newspaper. The residents' protests greatly distressed our people who had been actively serving the neighbourhood in community service since the church began. Finally, we identified a good site and began to prepare a plan for its development. It was a most suitable site, and I knew from my background in town planning it should satisfy the local municipality's criteria for traffic access and parking for a community facility. The challenge now was to lead our people in prayer to claim that site and its potential. We had to go to the public hearings in faith, not fear. As we listened to Hebrews 10:35—11:7 together, in an echo of Noah's daring, I reminded the congregation of what God was calling us to with the words:

> *God still calls us to build boats in dry paddocks,*
> *And save others through the chaos of flood.*

That is the point. It is God's call—and God's risk—to use us, and it is always for the sake of others. Of course, we will get a lot of satisfaction from realizing our potential through our creation and spiritual gifts, but we are invited to this courage of faith for others to benefit. On this occasion, God used my professional planning expertise and my preaching for a building project. Your experience and gifting will likely have a very different application and another setting, but it will take risky courage to respond.

THE SIN IS DISOBEYING, NOT BEING AFRAID

The fear of risk is not in itself the sin, but like the ten spies who saw the giants and refused to enter the Promised Land, fear may cause you to doubt God and disobey (Num 13; 14). If your fear comes from thinking what God is asking is too difficult, even with Holy Spirit power and intervention, you are doubting by not acting. We have the examples of Mary and Sarah who discovered through their miraculous pregnancies that with God, nothing is too difficult. Mary was told that by the angel (Luke 1:37). Sarah heard the Lord say it to her husband (Gen 18:14). She laughed, but found it to be true—nothing is too hard for God.

There were many times I hung on to that assurance as God's promise to me. It was not about a child for me as it was for Sarah and Mary, even though after seven years of marriage and two miscarriages, our son when he came was a special gift from God. (We named him "gift from God" to celebrate that.) For me, the promise offered reassurance that in midlife there would be a church where I could serve as a pastor. Whenever it seemed impossible, I revisited those words to Abraham and Sarah, "Is anything too hard for the Lord?" You may need to hear them often too.

UNDERSTAND YOUR FEAR

Australians do not generally have the same cultural fear of the sea that the Hebrews had. Most of us live around the coast and we are taught early to swim. We relish our beaches and surf and make a point of knowing all about rips, those vagaries of the ocean that carry you out into the deep. We learn the theory—do not try to swim against the flow but go with the rip until you get out of it further down the beach. But fear can overwhelm received wisdom. Twice I have been caught in a rip at nearby beaches and each time I have succumbed to the sudden panic, the helplessness, the awful tiredness when you realise you have been trying to get through the breakers for fifteen minutes and have made no progress. The realisation that you are the only one left in the water and everyone else is out on the beach watching you, does not help either.

So even though it has made me cautious about where and when we go into the water, especially when it is rough, we still swim daily in summer. Past experience of not achieving goals or feeling out of your depth may cause you the same reluctance to take a risk. If so, seek healing for those memories. A childhood blighted by neglect or rejection, can make fear of failure very real. Do not sink into bitterness or self-pity and shut yourself off from God, settling for less than you are called to. In grace this heavenly Father wants only the best for you and that applies to all your life, not just to finding your voice. As Mary Angelou has pointed out, courage is needed for every task of service to others. "One isn't necessarily born with courage, but one is born with potential. Without courage, we cannot practice any other virtue with consistency. We can't be kind, true, merciful, generous, or honest."[2]

So pray for courage, practice courage in small things, and seek help. And fuel your faith with God's promises.

---

2. Quoted by McGregor in "Maya Angelou on leadership."

FUELING YOUR FAITH

There are many examples of faith-filled courage in Scripture. We also find it in the biographies of other Christians and among our own friends and fellow pilgrims. Each of them can spur us on to live whole-heartedly in the same way they do. But though examples may encourage us, they do not give us the fuel for faith. Only learning to depend on God's promises grows our hope. In Rubem Alves words quoted at the beginning of this chapter, *hope* is the melody of the future, *faith* is to dance to it.

As I have pondered where God has brought me over these many years and given me the confidence to follow his leading, sometimes at considerable risk, I have gone back to the Psalms. I have read again and again the hope-filled verses that have jumped out at me at different intervals when I have felt ready to give up. My father modelled for me reading a psalm each morning and these heartfelt cries of confidence in God (and sometimes, of despair) have continued to grow my hope. In the early days, I just wrote the Bible verse in my diary without any comment about why it was significant for me that day. Later I learned to record *why* it spoke to me or what the issue was at the time. Reading back through these notes periodically has shown me how often God was preparing me for some decision that was to come, an action that would ask me to hang onto the word of promise already given, or to step out in faith, always depending on the Holy Spirit's power, not myself.

It was the kind of courage I admired in the pioneering missionary women I mentioned in the introduction to this book. These women had travelled in faith to far-flung regions of the world, and I delighted in their stories of different cultures as well as their personal journey with God. For a long time, I thought only those leaving their country were called upon to take such faith steps. I did not appreciate until much later the risks my parents and others had taken over the years to respond to God's call at home. But I came to see that in fact, all followers of Christ are invited to live this way of courage, wherever we are. It is the nature of being disciples. The writer to the Hebrews concludes his gallery of faith heroes with these words:

> Therefore, since we are surrounded by such a great cloud of witnesses, let us throw off everything that hinders and the sin that so easily entangles. And let us run with perseverance the race marked out for us, fixing our eyes on Jesus, the pioneer and perfecter of faith. For the joy set before him he endured the cross, scorning its shame, and sat down at the right hand of the throne of God (Heb 12:1–2).

How do can you counter fear with a grounded faith in God's promises? How can you act with courage in response to God's call? I have some final suggestions for you.

- When fear buffets you, slow down. Notice your reactions and realise what is happening. Choose neither fight nor flight.
- Continue to be still and experience God's presence with you. That changes you.
- Fix your eyes on Jesus. When you are looking at him, you are looking less on yourself and your fear. Choose some verses or songs to focus on his love for you.
- Ask Jesus to show you if something in your past experience is contributing to your fear. Surrender to his loving healing ministry.
- Then act in the courage of faith even if you are still afraid. Rely on the Holy Spirit to give you what you need.

Personal Reflection

As you find your voice and see what God is calling you to, whatever the season of your life, this passage from the Apostle Paul's letter to the Ephesians is my prayer for you:

> I ask—ask the God of our Master, Jesus Christ, the God of glory—to make you intelligent and discerning in knowing him personally, your eyes focused and clear, so that you can see exactly what it is he is calling you to do, grasp the immensity of this glorious way of life he has for his followers, oh, the utter extravagance of his work in us who trust him—endless energy, boundless strength! (Eph 1:17–19 The Message).

Epilogue

Mary's Story

Mary's *yes* to God's request for her to be the mother of the longed-for Messiah is a wonderful demonstration of courage and faith. This imagined retelling of Mary's story is in her words as I suppose they might sound in the twenty-first century. It is drawn from the first and second chapters of Luke's gospel in The Message paraphrase. Let it challenge you to also step out in God's plan and grasp the future offered to you.

I AM MARY.

I want to tell you my story, simply and honestly, and describe what made it possible for me to say "yes" to God's surprising request for me to carry to birth his son Jesus. Some people put me on a pedestal, even worship me or see me as a channel to God. On the other hand, for fear of this false worship, others do not talk much about me or do not see me as an ordinary human woman. But I am.

When I faced the tough call the day the angel came, I didn't have the advantage of looking back as I do now. But the Scriptures tell my story very straightforwardly, and that's what I want to do here. At that turning point in my life, I was only a teenager but already betrothed to Joseph as was the custom in my Palestine culture. This promise to marry was as binding as the wedding which followed it and to not go through with it would be like a divorce.

Joseph was established as a carpenter so older than me and a good man. Both of us looked eagerly for the coming of the Messiah—we were the kind of people who were called "the quiet of the land" because we lived faithfully and simply, waiting for God's promise of a national deliverer to be fulfilled. The song of delight I composed at the time expresses not only my joy in being chosen for this task but also a strong desire to see God's justice and power come to our world through this Messiah. I didn't know what having this baby would really mean. But my visionary song was in the tradition of the prophets and prophetesses of Israel who were looking forward to this time when our people would be delivered from oppression.

The day the angel appeared I was so afraid, as anybody would be. I later heard, so also was my cousin Zechariah when an angel appeared to him. God's messenger told me not to be afraid, but I couldn't help being shocked, especially as his first words were (as you would translate them today):

> Good morning!
> You're beautiful with God's beauty,
> Beautiful inside and out!
> God be with you.

Shaken, troubled—just an ordinary girl, and the angel says I'm beautiful! This word speaks of grace, God's gift which I didn't earn or work for. Made me wonder what was coming next! The angel must have seen this, so he says.

> Mary, you have nothing to fear. God has a surprise for you:
> You will become pregnant and give birth to a son and call his name Jesus.
> He will be great,
>   be called "Son of the Highest."
> The Lord God will give him
>   the throne of his father David.

Can't believe what I'm hearing—me? Part of God's plan for the Messiah—we long for him, but me? I realise now that God's way is always to lift us up—to realise the potential he has given us.

I needed to know the practicalities of this—I was indeed a virgin. I can testify that the Scriptures in Isaiah prophesying the coming of the Messiah through a virgin mean what they say. I was engaged but hadn't had sex yet with anyone, not even Joseph. So of course, I wanted to delicately ask, "How?"

God's angel was very patient with me. I guess God didn't want me to be like an unquestioning robot or just say yes without thinking. I could tell it was quite all right to ask "How?" when the angel replied:

> The Holy Spirit will come upon you,
> the power of the Highest hover over you;
> Therefore, the child you bring to birth
> will be called Holy, Son of God.

I should have known that questions about amazing things done in the supernatural realm always have the Holy Spirit as the answer to the "How?" But it's so easy to forget that. "Holy irregularity" someone has called it. Isn't that great? I like that! "Holy" because it is God's work, "irregularity" because it is out of the ordinary. I certainly wasn't expecting this.

But the wonderful thing is that God was not attempting to over-ride my consent. It was up to me to say yes or no. I suppose if I had said no then God would have chosen someone else because his plan for the world was much bigger than me. But what I would have missed out on!

Later on, when baby Jesus was born and we were in the temple dedicating him to God, Simeon, one of God's far-seeing people said that because of this child, a sword would pierce my heart. How true that was. I don't think anyone could imagine anything worse than standing at the foot of a Roman cross and seeing your son die there slowly, in great agony. Did I glimpse any of that on that day of the angel's visit? Maybe not, but I do know that God's plan for his world doesn't become a reality easily. Following God is not a bed of (how would you say it?), a bed of roses. God's gracious invitation to me that day was to join his son's mission in this world, and if that involved suffering, then I suppose I was deliberately choosing to be part of the suffering as well as the triumph.

But this was to be God's son. The result of the Holy Spirit coming on me. How did the biology work? I didn't really need to know. People down through the ages have had some funny ideas about this, mostly because they didn't understand how the human body worked. They thought women were gardens where men planted seed. A womb for hire, you might say. Even Luke, the doctor, writing my story doesn't elaborate on the biology of it, but Jesus later taught us he was indeed the God-man—both divine and human.

So though I didn't know how it would work, I did know God was inviting me to cooperate. God is the Creator, so naturally understands these things. And while I wondered aloud about it at the time, in the long run, I was prepared to accept God knew best. All I could do was trust.

Then there was the problem of how to tell Joseph. What would he make of his "virgin" wife suddenly pregnant before our marriage? He would have every right to divorce me—and in my society that would mean I would have no means of support and be disgraced and shunned—a life sentence. Apparently later the gossip was that I was having a child to a Roman soldier! This next hurdle though was in God's hands too. Perhaps he would send an angel to speak to Joseph. That would certainly help. But even if Joseph were accepting, I would still have to go through nine months of explaining to friends and family what was going on.

As it happened, God had some help for me in that too and the angel told me my cousin Elizabeth in the hill country was unexpectedly pregnant. I discovered when I got there that she was well along in her "miraculous" God-given pregnancy and because she was older and more mature than I, she was able to help me through those first difficult months. I found I could trust God with these practical matters.

The lesson I was learning is that I didn't need to worry about the impossible when God was involved. As the angel said about Elizabeth, "Nothing, you see, is impossible with God." So I said, "Yes." Simply accepted God's invitation to be the mother of the God-man.

Of course, it started with God's acceptance of me. That first greeting from the angel messenger was what made it possible for me to say "yes." Hearing I was acceptable to God gave me a profound and tough faith. I knew I might be putting aside personal hopes, facing disgrace, even possibly losing Joseph, and not having a normal marriage and family. It would involve challenging the status quo and suffering the consequences, even making mistakes in raising this special child. In fact, I did not always get it right and kept fussing over him well after he had become a man and was pursuing his mission.

But in accepting God's beautiful words, I was not being a doormat. When the going got tough, I would hear those words over and over again, "You are favored by God." Every day I could whisper "God loves me dearly" and listen for his voice calling me to my greatest potential as his obedient servant. I could pray, "O God, help me to believe your truth about myself no matter how impossible it is!"

Bibliography

Alves, Rubem. *Tomorrow's Child: Imagination, Creativity, and the Rebirth of Culture.* New York: Harper, 1972.
Angelou, Maya. *I Know Why the Caged Bird Sings.* Hachette Digital, 2010.
Bailey, Kenneth E. *Paul through Mediterranean Eyes: Cultural Studies in 1 Corinthians.* Downers Grove, IL: IVP, 2011. Kindle.
Baptist Union of Great Britain. *Patterns and Prayers for Christian Worship.* Oxford University Press, 1995.
Banks, Robert. *Redeeming the Routines: Bringing Theology to Life.* Grand Rapids, MI: Baker Academic, 1993.
Barton, Ruth Haley. *Strengthening the Soul of Your Leadership: Seeking God in the Crucible of Ministry.* Downers Grove, IL: IVP, 2012.
Bauman, Christy Angelle. *The Theology of the Womb: Knowing God through the Body of a Woman.* Eugene, OR: Cascade, 2019.
Beach, Nancy. *Gifted to Lead: The Art of Leading as a Woman in the Church.* Grand Rapids, MI: Zondervan, 2008.
Benner, David G. *The Gift of Being Yourself: The Sacred Call to Self-Discovery.* Downers Grove, IL: IVP, 2015.
Bonhoeffer, Dietrich. *Letters and Papers from Prison.* London: Fontana, 1951.
Brown, Brené. *Daring Greatly: How the Courage to be Vulnerable Transforms the Way we Live, Love, Parent, and Lead.* New York: Avery, 2012.
Bryson, Bill. *The Body: A Guide for Occupants.* Black Swan, 2020, Kindle.
Buechner, Frederick. *Listening to Your Life.* HarperSanFrancisco, 1992.
———. *Whistling in the Dark: An ABC Theologized.* San Francisco, CA: Harper and Row, 1988.
Clance, Pauline R. and Suzanne A. Imes. "The Impostor Phenomenon in High Achieving Women: Dynamics and Therapeutic Intervention." *Psychotherapy: Theory, Research and Practice.* 15 (3, 1978).
Crabb, Annabel. *The Wife Drought: Why Women Need Wives, and Men Need Lives.* North Sydney: Random House Australia, 2014.
Crabb, Larry. *Inside Out.* Colorado Springs, CO: NavPress, 1988.
Crick, Francis. *The Astonishing Hypothesis: The Scientific Search for the Soul.* London: Simon and Schuster, 1994.
Denny, Jenny, "If God Doesn't Hate My Body, Why Should I?" *Eternity* (Summer 2020): 20–22, Sydney, Australia: Bible Society Magazine.
Foster, Richard. *Money, Sex and Power.* London: Hodder and Stoughton, 1985.

Graham, Michelle. *Wanting to be Her: Body Image Secrets Victoria Won't Tell You.* Downers Grove, IL: IVP, 2005.
Harper, Lisa Sharon. *The Very Good Gospel: How Everything Wrong Can Be Made Right.* New York: WaterBrook, Penguin Random House, 2016.
Harris, Brian. *The Tortoise Usually Wins.* Milton Keynes, U.K.: Paternoster, 2013.
Hart, Archibald D. *Me, Myself, and I.* Guildford, U.K.: Highland, 1992.
Hill, Graham Joseph. *Holding up Half the Sky: A Biblical Case for Women Leading and Teaching in the Church.* Eugene, OR: Cascade, 2020.
Hill, Harriet, Margaret Hill, Richard Baggé, and Pat Miersma. *Healing the Wounds of Trauma: How the Church Can Help.* Exp. ed., Philadelphia, PA: American Bible Society, 2016.
Holliday, Brian and Beth Roberton, eds. *Epiphanies of Grace: Poems and Psalms from the Dayspring Community.* Dianella, Western Australia: Dayspring, 2011.
Ingram, Mark, ed. *Glimpses of Glory.* self-published, 2015.
Johns, Cheryl Bridges. *Seven Transforming Gifts of Menopause: An Unexpected Spiritual Journey.* Grand Rapids, MI: Brazos Press, 2020.
Johnson, Alan F. *How I Changed my Mind about Women in Leadership: Compelling Stories from Prominent Evangelicals.* Grand Rapids, MI: Zondervan, 2010.
Keller, Tim. *Identity, Business and the Christian Gospel.* Presentation, Acton Institute for the Study of Religion and Liberty, Grand Rapids, MI, 17 October 2018. https://www.youtube.com/watch?v=LUH-S6IP_Zg Accessed 24 April 2021.
———. *The Freedom of Self-forgetfulness: The Path to True Christian Joy.* Chorley, U.K.: 10Publishing, 2012.
Kristof, Nicholas D. and Sheryl WuDunn. *Half the sky: How to Change the World.* London: Hachette Digital, 2009. Kindle. Subsequently re-published with the subtitle: *Turning Oppression into Opportunity for Women Worldwide.*
Le Fevre, Perry, ed. *Prayers of Kierkegaard.* University of Chicago Press, 1956.
L'Engle, Madeleine. *The Ordering of Love.* Colorado Springs, CO: Shaw, 2005.
Leach, Tara Beth. *Emboldened: A Vision for Empowering Women in Ministry.* Downers Grove, IL: IVP, 2017.
Long, Michaela O'Donnell. *A Seat at the Table.* De Pree Center, Fuller Seminary. https://www.depree.org/workbooks/seat-at-the-table/ Accessed 24 April 2021.
McGahan, Anna. *Metanoia: A Memoir of a Body, Born Again.* Sydney, Australia: Acorn, 2019.
McGregor, Jena. "Maya Angelou on Leadership, Courage and the Creative Process." The Washington Post May 29, 2014 on the death of Maya Angelou. Original source for the quotation not identified.
McKnight, Scot. *The Heaven Promise.* London: Hodder and Stoughton, 2015.
Mangan, Susan. "Finding Awe in Uncertain Times." The Thrive Center, Fuller Seminary, 2020. https://www.thethrivecenter.org/finding-awe-in-uncertain-times Accessed 24 April 2021.
Miles, Margaret M. *Fulness of Life.* Philadelphia, PA: Westminster, 1981.
Mulholland Jr., M. Robert and Ruth Haley Barton. *Invitation to a Journey: A Road Map for Spiritual Formation.* Downers Grove, IL: IVP, 2016.
O'Connor, Elizabeth. *Journey Inward, Journey Outward.* New York: Harper and Row, 1968.

Ortberg, John. *If you Want to Walk on Water, you Have to Get out of the Boat*. Grand Rapids, MI: Zondervan, 2001. Now republished with resources for a 6-session journey on learning to trust God.

Packer, J. I. *Knowing God*. 20th Anniversary Edition, Downers Grove, IL: IVP, 1993.

Piper, John. *Rethinking Retirement: Finishing Life for the Glory of Christ*. Wheaton, IL: Crossway, 2008.

Robinson, Martin. *Sacred Places, Pilgrim Paths: An Anthology of Pilgrimage*. London: Fount-HarperCollins, 1998.

Rohr, Richard. *Falling Upward: A Spirituality for the Two Halves of Life*. San Francisco, CA: Jossey-Bass, 2011.

Sandberg, Sheryl. *Lean In: Women, Work, and the Will to Lead*. London, U.K.: WH Allen, 2015.

Sayers, Dorothy L. *Are Women Human? Penetrating, Sensible and Witty Essays on the Role of Women in Society*. Grand Rapids, MI: Eerdmans, 1971.

Smedes, Lewis B. *Shame and Grace: Healing the Shame we Don't Deserve*. Grand Rapids, MI: Zondervan, 1993.

Turley, Bruce. *Turning Points: An Invitation to Growth and Healing*. Melbourne, Australia: JBCE, 1985.

Turner, Jennifer. "Let's Get Physical: On Keeping Body and Soul Together." *Zadok Perspectives*, 46 (September 1994): 12–13.

———. "Letting Go . . ." *Zadok Perspectives* 53 (Winter 1996): 12–13.

———. "Naked in Eden." *Zadok Perspectives* 48 (March 1995): 16–17.

———. "Shame!" *Zadok Perspectives* 27 (September 1989): 17.

———. "Theology of Everyday Life." In *Vose Seminary at 50*. eds. Nathan Hobby, et al., 212–217. Preston, Victoria, Australia: Mosaic, 2013.

Turner, Jennifer, and Mark Ingram, eds. *Life in the Spirit: Writings of Dr E.G. Gibson*. Osborne Park, Western Australia: Vocational Education and Training Publications, 2009.

Ward, Adrian F. "The Neuroscience of Everyone's Favorite Topic: Why Do People Spend So Much Time Talking About Themselves?" *Scientific American* 309 (16 July 2013): 1.

Willard, Dallas. *Renovation of the Heart: Putting on the Character of Christ*. Colorado Springs, CO: NavPress, 2002. Kindle.

———. *The Spirit of the Disciplines: Understanding how God Changes Lives*. New York: Harper Collins, 1991.

Williamson, Marianne. *A Return to Love: Reflections on the Principles of a Course in Miracles*. New York: Harper Collins, 1992.

Woodlock, Janet. "Vocational Discernment and Female Experience of Pastoral Ministry Call." *Zadok Papers* S232 (Spring 2018): 8–16.

Wright, N. T. *God and the Pandemic: A Christian Reflection on the Coronavirus and its Aftermath*. London: SPCK, 2020.

———. *Surprised by Hope*. London: SPCK, 2007.

Yancey, Philip. *Soul Survivor: How my Faith Survived the Church*. London: Hodder and Stoughton, 2001.

www.ingramcontent.com/pod-product-compliance
Lightning Source LLC
Chambersburg PA
CBHW050824160426
43192CB00010B/1882